SOUTH-INDIAN IMAGES
OF
GODS AND GODDESSES

SOUTH-INDIAN IMAGES
OF
GODS AND GODDESSES

BY

H. KRISHNA SASTRI, B.A., RAO SAHEB,
Assistant Archaeological Superintendent for Epigraphy,
Southern Circle

Published under the authority of the Government of Madras

GYAN

Published by

GYAN

Gyan Publishing House
5, Ansari Road
Daryaganj, New Delhi-110002
Phone: 011-47034999, 9811692060
E-mail: books@gyanbooks.com

Distribution Network
gyanbooks.com
India, USA, Canada, UK, Australia, France

ISBN : 978-81-212-2610-3 (HB)
First Published, 1916

2nd Impression 2021

Printed at: Gyan Press, Delhi.

South-Indian Images of Gods and Goddesses
Author: H. Krishna Sastri

SOUTH-INDIAN IMAGES

OF

GODS AND GODDESSES

BY

H. KRISHNA SASTRI, B.A., RAO SAHEB,

Assistant Archæological Superintendent for Epigraphy, Southern Circle.

Published under the authority of the Government of Madras.

MADRAS GOVERNMENT PRESS.

1916.

THE TANJORE TEMPLE.

PREFACE.

THIS little book owes its origin to a suggestion made by His Excellency Lord Carmichael, when he was Governor of Madras in the year 1912. He felt that, while there was a multitude of books dealing with Hindu religion and incidentally with Hindu iconography, there was no popular handbook which would give information about the images one commonly sees in temples or museums in Southern India, and that it would be a distinctly useful thing to supply that want. The Madras Government entrusted the task to me, presumably because my official duties bring me very often to visit the various temples in the Province and to study and classify the images found therein.

When I accepted the task, I was not fully aware of the difficulties that lay before me. In the first place, there were very few printed books, in Sanskrit or in translations, that gave the orthodox description and significance of the images set up in temples. And when I managed to collate notes from a few old manuscripts treating of this subject, it was almost impossible in several instances to reconcile the discrepancies which they showed or even to understand the technical terms which abounded in them. In some cases, the description of a particular image found in the local chronicles or *Sthala-Purānas* could not be traced in the *Āgamas*. I am not altogether sanguine that I have steered clear of these difficulties and succeeded in presenting a clear and readable account to the average reader.

My chief source of information in compiling this book has been an excellent work entitled "Tattvanidhi," published by the Srī-Venkatēsvara Steam Press at Bombay, and compiled by His Highness the Mahārāja Mummadi Krishnarāja Vodeyar Bahadūr of Mysore. A short bibliography of other Sanskrit works consulted by me is given at page xv.

Among the many friends who have kindly helped me in this task, my special thanks are due to Sir J. H. Marshall, *Kt.*, C.I.E., M.A., LITT.D., F.S.A., Director-General of Archæology, Simla, and his assistant Mr. V. Natesa Aiyar, B.A., for extracts from ancient manuscripts on the subject of Indian iconography; to Mr. A. H. Longhurst, Archæological Superintendent, Southern Circle, for the numerous illustrations without which the book would be almost unintelligible; and to Mr. C. S. Anantarama Aiyar, the Under Secretary to the Government of Madras, for much valuable criticism which has been of great assistance to me. My thanks are also due to Mr. T. Fisher, Superintendent, Government Press, Madras, for his many kind suggestions about the get-up of the book and a practical arrangement of the numerous illustrations.

OOTACAMUND,
1st April 1916.

H. KRISHNA SASTRI.

TABLE OF CONTENTS.

CHAPTER I.

INTRODUCTORY.

CHAPTER II.

BRAHMA.

CHAPTER III.

VISHNU.

CHAPTER IV.

SIVA.

CHAPTER V.

SAKTI-GODDESSES.

CHAPTER VI.

VILLAGE DEITIES.

CHAPTER VII.

MISCELLANEOUS DEITIES.

LIST OF ILLUSTRATIONS.

SANSKRIT BOOKS CONSULTED.

Mayamata.
Mānasāra.
Chaturvargachintāmaṇi (Hēmādri).
Brihatsamhitā (Varāhamihira).
Kāsyapa-Silpa (from the Bhānumat or Amsumat-Tantra).
Brāhmīya-Silpa.
Silparatna.
Silpasangraha.
Silpasāra.
Tattvanidhi (with numerous quotations; printed at the Srī-Venkatesvara Steam Press, Bombay).
Sabdakalpadruma (the Encyclopædia of Sanskrit Literature by Rājā Rādhākānta Deo; printed in Calcutta).
Bhāgavata-Purāna.

SOUTH-INDIAN IMAGES OF

GODS AND GODDESSES

CHAPTER I.

INTRODUCTORY.

I

Almost every village of any importance in Southern India has its temple, round which centres in a very large measure the corporate civic life of the community which lives in it. The casual visitor is at once attracted by the temple and when he goes there he sees various images in all sorts of incongruous postures and is generally puzzled to know what they mean or what they represent, and how they serve to evoke the religious feelings of the people worshipping them. An attempt will be made in the succeeding pages to describe and classify them in various groups so as to make them more intelligible to the ordinary visitor.

Elaborate rules have been laid down in the ancient *Āgamas* and *Silpa-Sāstras* as to the place where temples are to be built, the kinds of images to be installed there, the materials with which such images are to be fashioned, and even the dimensions and proportions of various kinds of images, to vary which will result in untold calamity to the maker and the worshipper alike. The curious reader may, for example, refer to *Sukranitisāra* (Chapter IV, Section IV, verses 130 et seq.).[1]

II

Temples must have existed in this part of the country from time immemorial. But the earliest inscriptional evidence of the existence of temples takes us back only to the age of the Pallava kings, which is supposed to be between the fourth

[1] Pages 166 to 182 of Vol. XIII of the "Sacred Books of the East" series, published by the Pānini Press, Allahabad.

and the ninth centuries of the Christian era.[1] The more ancient temples were probably made of wood and other such perishable material, as we find to this day in parts of Malabar. Perhaps the Pallavas were among the very first in Southern India to build temples of durable material. In fact one of the most famous of these Pallava kings, Mahēndravarman I, who reigned about the beginning of the seventh century A.D., was known by the title *Chetthakāri*, i.e., the maker of *chaityas* or temples.[2]

The earliest Pallava monuments so far discovered are those of Mahābalipuram or the Seven Pagodas. They consist of solid *rathas* cut out of a single rock and of temples scooped out of the living boulder. The form of these *rathas* and temples served perhaps as models to the later temples in cut stone, such as those of the Shore Temple there, the Kailāsanātha and Vaikuntha-Perumāl temples at Conjeeveram, and other Pallava temples elsewhere.

III

The Pallavas were succeeded by the Chōla kings, who are justly entitled to be regarded as the greatest temple-builders of Southern India. About 90 per cent of the temples now found were erected in their time. They are generally dedicated either to Siva or Vishnu, and in their simplest form consist of a cell called the *Garbha-griha*,—the central shrine, surmounted by a spire or dome, with a hall in front, called *Mukha-mandapa* and a narrow passage or vestibule connecting the two, called the *Ardha-mandapa*, which is open on two sides to permit of the priestly worshippers circumambulating the central shrine. In the *Mukha-mandapa* or just outside it will be placed the image of the deity's chief vehicle, the Nandi-bull in Siva temples and the Garuda-bird in Vishnu temples. This is generally the limit up to which the non-Brahman classes are allowed to come. Round and outside of these are the *Mahā-mandapa*, the big hall, and other pavilions in which on special occasions processional images of the deity are placed and worshipped. Next after the *Mahā-mandapa* there will be two raised platforms, one behind the other, on one

[1] The Buddhist *stūpas* at Amarāvatī and other villages in the Guntūr district, the *stūpa* at Sankaram in the Vizagapatam district, and the caverns with rock-cut beds in the Madura and Tinnevelly districts are certainly much older but cannot in any sense be called temples. Some of these last may, however, have been used as temples in a much later period either by Buddhists or by Jainas.

[2] Simultaneously with Mahēndravarman I, in the Pallava dominions, rock-cut temples appear to have come into existence in the Pāndya and the Chēra (Kongu) countries under the patronage of their respective sovereigns.

of which is planted the flagstaff or *dhvaja-stambha*, made of stone, wood or metal, and on the other is offered what is called the *Sribali*, when sacrificial cooked food and flowers are offered to the minor divinities or powers who have to be appeased in order to ward off all evil and to prevent disturbance to the ordinary conduct of the daily worship. It is only up to this limit that foreigners are allowed to enter the temples by the orthodox Hindu.

In temples of any importance there will be a separate shrine for the goddess, but generally on a smaller scale than that of the chief deity. There are separate places for the kitchen where the offerings are prepared with scrupulous regard to ceremonial purity; there are storehouses where the articles required for a year's consumption in the temple are stored; and there is generally a fresh water well which is often the best source of drinking water in the village. The whole group of buildings is surrounded by high *prākāra* walls, whose gateways are surmounted by the characteristic towers (figs. 1 and 2) which lend distinction to a temple city. In some cases there will be outside the temple a big pleasure tank (fig. 3), generally square in size, built round with stone steps on all sides, and with a central *mandapa*, where once a year the god and goddess are taken in procession for the floating festival.

IV

The outer walls and the lofty flagstaff will easily show to the sight-seer whether the temple is dedicated to a Saiva divinity or to a Vaishnava god. In the former there will be seen images of the Nandi-bull in a recumbent posture, while the latter will show similar images of the Garuda-bird. Temples other than those of Siva and Vishnu are not uncommon and can easily be identified by similar marks of the characteristic vehicle of the god. Vishnu temples may also show the symbols of the conch and the discus and the caste mark *(nāmam)* of the Vaishnavas painted on the walls.

V

The ritual followed every day in the temples of Siva and Vishnu may be generally described as *rājōpachāra*, or the paying of royal honours. Thus in rich temples there will be elephants and camels with their appropriate paraphernalia, the royal umbrellas and *chauris* mounted on gold or silver handles, palanquins and other vehicles, a troupe of dancers and musicians, a host of other temple servants to wash the god, anoint him with sandal or decorate him with flowers and

FIG. 1.—*Gōpura*, Narasimha temple; Mangalagiri.

FIG. 2.—Back view of central shrine, Siva temple: Gangaikondasolapuram.

FIG. 3.—Haridrânadi tank; Mannârgudi.

so on. Crowns and other rich and costly jewellery, set with gems and pearls (fig. 4), and often presented by Rājas and Chieftains or other rich devotees, are a special pride of the wealthier temples.

The Brāhmana priest is to purify himself by bath and prayers early morning, and then open the doors of the sanctum and gently wake up the god, who is supposed to be sleeping, by chanting appropriate hymns in his praise. Then, after duly worshipping the guardian deities, he washes the feet of the chief deity, bathes the image, clothes it properly, decorates it with the usual jewellery, sandal and flowers, waving incense and lamps of diverse pattern (fig. 5) in front of the god and finally offering him the cooked food or *naivēdyam* and the final betel leaf and nut. At stated intervals the god comes out in procession and perhaps sees to the comfort of his attendant deities. Usually there is an important annual festival, representing in some cases the marriage of the god or some other special event in the doings of the god registered in local chronicles or *Purānas*. On such occasions the procession is carried on different vehicles, both common and special, the latter being such as the *kalpa-vriksha*, the wish-giving celestial tree or the *kāmadhēnu*, the wish-giving celestial cow, or the mythic animal *gandabhērunda*. The most important procession will generally be the car festival when the god goes round in the huge car through the main streets where his worshippers live and receives worship and offerings at their very homes.

VI

In the temples dedicated to the village deities the ceremonial is not much different. Brāhmanas however rarely officiate and animal sacrifices are generally offered, especially when the village is threatened with an epidemic or with serious scarcity or famine. Vedic incantations are not uttered in these temples.

With this brief general description of the temple, we can now proceed to study the various images which are found represented in them.

FIG. 4.—Processional images (metal); Madura.

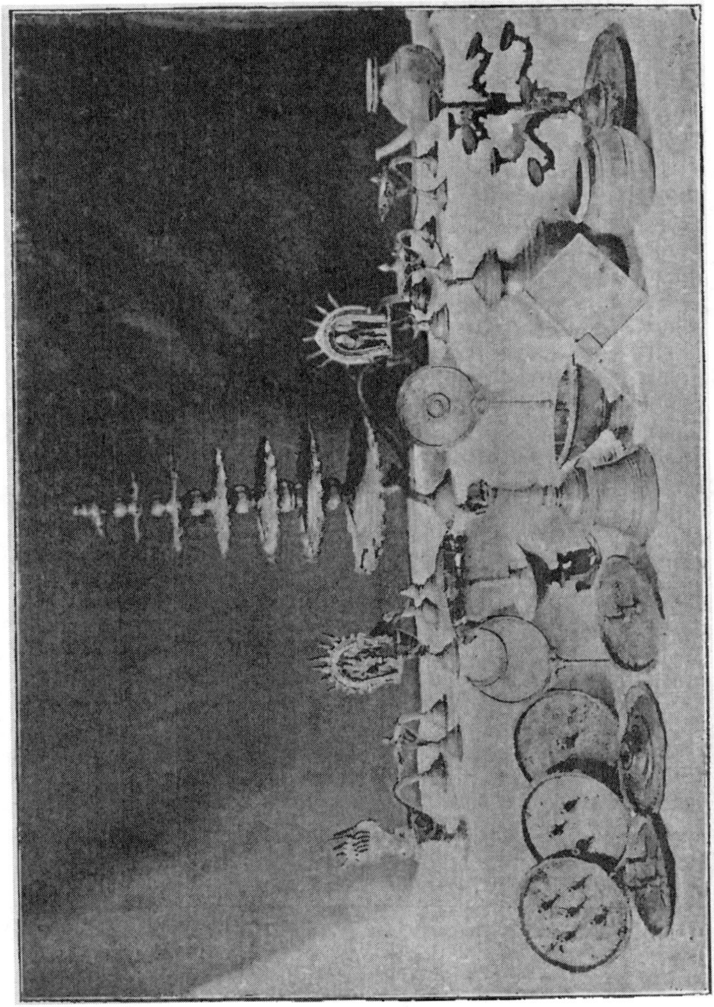

FIG. 5.—Lamp patterns and *pūjā*-utensils; Ūttattūr.

CHAPTER II.

BRAHMĀ.

Brahmā, distinct from Brahman, the all-pervading Eternal Spirit, is the first member of the Hindu Triad. His principal function is creation. Independent shrines dedicated to him are rather rare. Still, figures of this god are commonly found decorating one of the niches in the north wall of the central shrine in a Siva temple. Images of Brahmā may sometimes also be seen on pillars, ceilings or other parts of a temple; but the one point that deserves to be noted is that though often pictured the god is not worshipped[1] as the chief deity in a temple, like the two other members of the Triad, Vishnu and Siva.

BRAHMĀ-images; general type.

According to *Mānasāra*, one of the standard works on sculpture, Brahmā is represented with four heads. He has, however, only one body and four hands. The image may be standing or seated and made of metal or of stone. The palm of the left lower hand exhibits the posture of conferring boons *(varada)* while the right lower indicates protection *(abhaya)*. The corresponding upper hands hold the water-pot *(kamandalu)* and the rosary *(akshamālā)* or sometimes the sacrificial ladle *(srik)* and spoon *(sruva)*. The following ornaments are seen in a finished picture of Brahmā:—(1) ear-rings or pendants fashioned like the face of a crocodile; (2) the sacred thread *yajnasūtra* hanging right across the body from above the left shoulder; (3) the scarf *(uttariya)* thrown round the neck so as to stretch down to the knees; (4) the *udarabandhana*[2] or literally, a girdle going round the belly; (5) necklace and torque; (6) armlets, arm-rings, wristlets, anklets, waist-zone, finger-rings set with gems, etc. His hair is made

---

[1] According to the Brahmavaivarta-*Purāna* he was cursed by Mōhinī not to receive any worship; see also below, p. 93. In the Telugu and Canarese districts we occasionally find temples dedicated to Traipurusha, i.e., the three gods Brahmā, Vishnu and Siva. Curiously enough the place of Brahmā is here occupied by Sūrya, the Sun-god; see Babu Nagendra Natha Vasu's *Mayūrabhanja*, p. xxiv. From the *Nrisimhaprāsāda* quoted in *Tattvanidhi* we learn that one variety of Brahmā is of the form of Sun-god.

[2] In the Tanjore inscriptions this ornament is mentioned as made of gold and set with gems; see, e.g., *South-Indian Inscriptions*, Vol. II, p. 189.

up in the fashion known as *jatā-makuta* and he is attended by the two goddesses[1] Sarasvatī (on the right) and Sāvitrī (on the left).

Another representation shows Brahmā riding on a chariot drawn by seven swans *(hamsa*[2]*)*. His right lower hand rests on the palm of the left lower, the two other hands holding the usual rosary and the water-pot. He is seated on a full blown lotus-flower, with his eyes closed in a meditative posture. The goddess Sāvitrī is seated on his left thigh.[3] There are various other representations of Brahmā drawn purely from the imagination of the sculptor or painter and sometimes also based on *Purānic* legends. But the mainpoints which distinguish Brahmā from the other gods are the same in all. Hēmādri mentions some forms of Brahmā such as Prajāpati, Visvakarma,[4] Lōkapāla and Dharma. It may be noted that the swan vehicle and the goddesses are rarely, if at all, found in the figures of Brahmā generally set up in South-Indian temples. Various forms.

An old picture of Brahmā from Seven Pagodas (fig. 6) and a later one from Kumbakōnam (fig. 7) illustrate the standing posture described above. In the latter the left lower hand rests freely on the waist of the god and does not show the posture of conferring boons. The sitting attitude of Brahmā surmounted by a parasol and *chauris*—the symbols of supreme power—is beautifully illustrated by a picture from Tiruvādi near Tanjore (fig. 8). Another figure, which is unfortunately mutilated, shows the same position, but includes the standing figure of Sarasvatī on the right side of Brahmā (fig. 9). It is noticeable that in this figure the right upper hand of Brahmā is made to hold a lotus instead of the usual rosary. An image from Chidambaram (fig. 10) shows Brahmā on his swan vehicle folding two of his hands in a worshipping posture and holding the rosary and water-pot in the other two. Illustrations.

---

[1] For a description of these goddesses, see below, pp. 185 f. and 218, note 3. The Kālikā-*Purāna* mentions also the two goddesses, the ghee-pot on the left and the Vēdas in front, together with a number of attendant sages engaged in meditation.

[2] The conventional bird *hamsa* is represented in Hindu sculpture with a high neck, a crest *(stūpi)* on its head, white body, red feet and a beak of golden yellow.

[3] Brahmā with Sāvitrī on his left side, is called Prajāpati-Brahmā. He has only one face and no swan vehicle.

[4] Visvakarma has ten hands and holds the characteristic symbols of the three gods Brahmā, Vishnu and Mahēsvara. One of his symbols mentioned in the *Silpasāra* is the *māna-danda*, 'measuring rod.' He rides on an elephant and has his body besmeared with ashes. Another such god, who partakes of the nature of all the three gods, is the Sun. Still another is Dattātrēya who granted the objects of his desire to sage Atri. He is represented as a wandering mendicant with ashes rubbed over his body and followed by the four Vēdas in the form of four dogs. Dattātrēya is considered to be a form of Vishnu.

FIG. 6.—Brahmā ; Seven Pagodas.

FIG. 7.—Brahmā; Kumbakōnam.

FIG. 8.—Brahmā; Tiruvādi.

FIG. 9.—Brahmā and Sarasvatī; Kandiyūr.

FIG. 10.—Brahmā on swan vehicle; Chidambaram.

CHAPTER III.

VISHNU.

I

Vishnu is the second member of the Hindu Triad. His principal function is that of the protector of the universe. He is worshipped in South-Indian temples in various forms and under various names. The general description of Vishnu without reference to any of his particular incarnations is given in the *Mānasāra* as follows :—He has four arms and two eyes, wears a high crown and a yellow scarf; on his breast is the auspicious mark *Srīvatsa*; he holds the discus and the conch in his upper arms and the club and the sword (or lotus) in the lower and wears the garland *(vanamālā)* of flowers, reaching down to the knees. In some cases the lower arms exhibit the protecting and the boon-conferring postures (fig. 11).[1] A prominent nose, broad eyes and smiling countenance are other features of Vishnu. The goddesses Srī or Lakshmī (wealth) and Mahī or Prithvī (Earth) are usually represented on his right and left sides respectively.[2] The discus is generally held in the right hand and the conch in the left; but this arrangement is reversed in the case of an image found in the Bellary district (fig. 12). According to the *Kāsyapa-Silpa* the left lower hand of Vishnu may, without showing the *varada* or boon-conferring posture, rest on his waist freely (fig. 13) and the goddesses need not always be represented with him. Figures of Vishnu may be seen standing, seated or reclining. They receive different names in their different postures; but the Vaishnava symbols, viz., the discus and conch, the garland *vanamālā* and the auspicious mark *Srīvatsa* always remain the distinguishing features of Vishnu. Fig. 14

---

[1] This figure shows, however, four more hands holding a bow and arrow and a sword and shield.

[2] For a description of these goddesses, see below, p. 187. The *Pāncharātrāgama* mentions also the goddess Nīlādēvī and describes her as seated with four hands in two of which she holds lotus flowers.

FIG. 11.—Vishnu (Ashtabhuja); Conjeeveram.

FIG. 12.—Vishnu; Bellary.

FIG. 13.—Vishnu; Paramesvaramangalam.

FIG. 14.—Vishnu and his consorts ; Ariyanbākkam.

from Āriyambākkam in the Chingleput district illustrates the sitting form of Vishnu with the goddesses Srī and Bhū and two kneeling devotees.

II

His ten incarnations.

The more popular forms of Vishnu, worshipped in the temples, generally refer to his numerous *avatārs* or incarnations. There are ten such *avatārs* recognized as of primary importance; but of these only five are commonly represented for worship. They are (1) Varāha "the Boar incarnation"; (2) Narasimha "the Man-lion incarnation"; (3) Vāmana "the Dwarf incarnation," developing eventually into Trivikrama; (4) Rāma, the hero of the *Rāmāyana*; and (5) Krishna, the pastoral god and the chief actor in the great war of the *Mahābhārata*. The other five incarnations of Vishnu, viz., the Fish, the Tortoise, Parasurāma, Buddha and Kalki though represented largely on walls, pillars and ceilings of temples being either carved or painted, are not generally worshipped as the chief deity in a temple.[1]

III

VARAHA or Boar incarnation.

Varāha, also known as Ādivarāha, Dharanīvarāha or Bhūvarāha, is beautifully illustrated by the image in the Varāha-Perumāl cave-temple at Mahabalipuram. Here the boar-faced Vishnu is seen standing with his right foot resting on the hood of the serpent-god Sēsha. On the right thigh is seated the goddess Earth,[2] supported in position by the two lower arms of the god. He wears a high crown and has in his two upper hands the discus (held sideways) and the conch. As these images however have recently been covered with a thin coating of plaster and painted fantastically in variegated colours, it is not possible to say what sculptural peculiarities the original may have exhibited. Fortunately, a panel representing this same Varāha-*avatār* of Vishnu (fig. 15) with attendant deities, is found in another rock-cut *mandapa* at that village and is decidedly a true copy of the sculptures

---

[1] Parasurâma, "the axe-bearer, Râma" is supposed to be the founder of the west-coast country, having miraculously reclaimed it from the encroaching sea. He is, therefore, often worshipped in Malabar in special shrines dedicated to him. Siva temples with the name Parasurāmēsvara are common and these are believed to owe their existence to Parasurâma. In the Kachchhapēsvara temple at Conjeeveram, on a stone set up under a tree, there is a representation of the Tortoise incarnation of Vishnu, worshipping Siva. This is reproduced by Mr. Rea in his Madras Archæological Survey Report for 1910-11, Plate V, fig. 1.

[2] The *Brāhmīya-Silpa* states that Lakshmī (i.e. Srī) is also to be depicted on the side of Varāha.

FIG. 15.—Boar incarnation of Vishnu ; Seven Pagodas.

found in the shrine of the Varāha-Perumāl cave-temple. The scene depicts the primeval Boar rescuing from the depths of the ocean the goddess Earth, who had been kidnapped thither by the demon Hiranyāksha, an enemy of the gods. Sēsha, on whose wide-spread hoods the earth is generally supposed to rest, is also represented as rising from the ocean along with the Boar-god. He is folding his hands in the attitude of worship. The *dēvas* worshipping the god from above, the sages on the right, and Brahmā and Siva on the left indicate the joy felt by the entire universe on this occasion. This representation exactly follows the description given by Hēmādri in his *Chaturvarga-Chintāmani*. The hand with the discus is sometimes also shown as raised in the act of killing Hiranyāksha. The god may be represented as smiling after having killed Hiranyāksha and revived him by divine grace. Figures of the Man-boar in meditation or of a full Boar digging the earth in the midst of many demons, are also sometimes represented. In the pictures of Lingōdbhava (Siva) noted in the sequel, is seen the full Boar form of Vishnu digging the earth.

Temples dedicated to the Boar-incarnation of Vishnu are not many. This incarnation was a particular favourite of the Western Chalukya kings in the early centuries of the Christian era. A fine sculpture of Varāha carrying the goddess Earth is found in the Chalukyan rock-cut temple at Bādāmi (*Ind. Ant.*, Vol. VI, p. 354).[1] In later times, too, the Kākatīyas, the Reddis of Kondavīdu and the Hindu sovereigns of Vijayanagara, paid particular reverence to Varāha, adopting the boar as their royal crest. At Srīmushnam in the South Arcot district is a beautiful big temple dedicated to this god and so also is another at Tiruvadandai near Mahābalipuram in the Chingleput district.

IV

NARASIMHA or the Man-lion incarnation.

Narasimha or Nrisimha, the Man-lion is more popular than Varāha. A large number of families in the south, Brahman and non-Brahman, own him as their tutelary deity. In Tamil, the name is corrupted into Singa (Sanskrit *Simha*) or Singa-Perumāl, and in the other vernaculars into Narasa (a contraction of Narasimha). The story of this incarnation of Vishnu is briefly as follows:—

Hiranyāksha and Hiranyakasipu were two demon brothers, naturally hostile to Vishnu. Hiranyāksha was killed

[1] See also *Visvakarma*, Part VI, No. 99.

FIG. 16.—Narasimha bursting forth from the pillar ; Ahōbalam.

by Vishnu in his Varāha-*avatār*. Hiranyakasipu then became the king of the demons and vowed eternal war with Vishnu. His young son, Prahlāda, however, became a devoted adherent of Vishnu and was always praising him as the all-pervading lord of the universe. Exasperated with this, Hiranyakasipu asked the young boy whether his god Vishnu, if he was all-pervasive, could be found in the pillar in front of him; and then hacked at it with his sword. The pillar cleft in twain and out burst from it, to the astonishment of Hiranyakasipu, the angry god in the shape of a Man-lion, (fig. 16), who forthwith tore to pieces the impious demon king.

UGRA-NARASIMHA.

The angry god is called Ugra (the terrible)-Narasimha (figs. 17 and 18). When, however, his anger subsided at the earnest prayers of Prahlāda he became serene and in this form he is known as Lakshmī-Narasimha. Yōga-Narasimha (fig. 19) is another form in which the god is seen squatting in a meditative mood. Simhāchalam in the Vizagapatam district, Ahōbalam in the Kurnool district and Nāmakkal[1] in the Trichinopoly district may be mentioned among the places sacred to Narasimha. The usual Vaishnava symbols, *sankha* (conch) and *chakra* (discus), are seen in the two upper hands of the image of Narasimha in all his forms. The monolithic Ugra-Narasimha found in the ruins of Vijayanagara was there established by king Krishnarāya in A.D. 1528. It may be noted that here the god, though called Ugra-Narasimha, is not represented, as may be expected, in the posture of splitting open the bowels of the demon Hiranyakasipu.

LAKSHMĪ-NARASIMHA; YŌGA-NARASIMHA.

Hēmādri states that Narasimha must be represented with muscular shoulders, a stout neck and a slender waist. Half man and half lion, his face must be fiery and so also the mane round it. Standing with his right foot bent forward (*ālīdha*) he splits with his sharp nails the breast of the tyrant Hiranyakasipu, who, as the wise men say, is an embodiment of ignorance. The *Pāncharātrāgama* thus describes the form of Narasimha suited for meditation:—" (Terrible) like flaming fire, he has a lion-face with a human body, furious fangs, a protruding tongue, an open mouth, a thick mane and muscular chest. He stands in the *ālidha* posture in an angry mood and splits the breast of the giant, thrown flat upon his thigh, with the sharp nails of both his hands. In his two other hands he holds the symbols of the club and the discus." The *Mayamata*, while giving almost

---

[1] A detailed description of the images in the rock-cut temples at Nāmakkal is given in the Madras Epigraphical Report for 1906, Part II, pp. 75 and 76.

FIG 17.—Ugra-Narasimha ; Ahôbalam.

FIG. 18.—Ugra-Narasimha (metal) ; Madras Museum.

FIG. 19.—Yōga-Narasimha ; Tirupati Hill.

the same description of him, states that the cruel form of Narasimha is installed on mountain-tops, caves, forests or the enemy's territory when the enemy has to be destroyed; when installed, however, in villages and towns he has four hands, two of which wear the conch and the discus.

V

VĀMANA or the Dwarf incarnation.

Vāmana or the Dwarf incarnation of Vishnu is worshipped in its ultimate manifestation, under the Sanskrit name Trivikrama or the Tamil Ulagalanda-Perumāl. The former means "the god who took three strides" and the latter "the lord who measured the universe (with three strides)."

The story is that a powerful demon king named Bali, the great-grandson of Hiranyakasipu mentioned above, conquered the three worlds and ruled them, in spite of his birth, in charity and with justice. Indra, the chief of gods, was thus superseded. Vishnu as the avowed destroyer of the demons *(dānavas)* and the upholder of the gods had to restore Indra to his legitimate position. Vishnu could not go to war against Bali, as he was a virtuous king. So he went in the guise of a Dwarf Brāhmana, a student of the Vēdas *(brahmachārin)*, and begged of Bali for three feet of land on which he could sit and meditate on Brahman undisturbed. The generous Bali granted the request. But what was his astonishment when he saw the cunning god grow to a height transcending the world, take in at one step the whole earth, covering the sky

TRIVIKRAMA.

with the next, and demanding of Bali to show him room for the third. True to his promise, Bali offered his own head, on which the god placed his foot and sent him down to the lower regions. Greatly pleased with the king's nobility and firmness of character, Vishnu is still supposed to be guarding as his servant the palace of Bali in the world below.

There are not many temples dedicated to this god. At Tirukkoyilur in the South Arcot district is a celebrated shrine of Trivikrama. Another one is the Ulagalanda-Perumāl temple at Kānchī. In the Varāha-*mandapa* at Mahābalipuram, on the panel opposite to the Varāha-*avatār* described above, is a fine representation of Trivikrama[1] (fig. 20). Here the god has eight hands. The foremost arm on the right side is artistically made to support the lintel, while the remaining three hold the discus, club and the sword. Of the arms on the left side two hold the bow and the shield;

[1] There is also a panel in the rock-cut temple at Nāmakkal, representing Trivikrama with more details.

FIG. 20.—Trivikrama ; Seven Pagodas.

the third has the conch and the fourth is pointed towards Brahmā seated on the lotus. This Brahmā has four hands and four faces (?). He reverently touches with one of his hands the toe of the uplifted leg of Trivikrama and with another touches the finger of the god pointed towards him. On the corresponding right side of Trivikrama is found apparently Siva, also on a lotus-seat. The Sun and Moon, with circles of light behind their heads, perhaps to distinguish their respective functions, are seen flying in the air half way down the high face of the god. Two other heavenly beings, one of which is on a level with the head of Trivikrama and has a horse-face,[1] are also flying in the air. The seated figures at the foot of Trivikrama are apparently Bali and his retinue who are struck with amazement at the sudden transformation of the stunted Vāmana into the all-pervading Trivikrama. In the Rāmasvāmin temple at Kumbakōnam is a sculptured pillar (fig. 21) on which the story of the Vāmana-*avatār* is well represented. The lower section shows Bali and his wife granting boons to Brāhmanas. In the upper section is the god Trivikrama under a floral arch. His right foot is placed in the two open palms of the Earth. On his right is the image of the Dwarf. His vehicle Garuda is behind him. On the left side are evidently Bali and his wife standing. This description of Trivikrama exactly coincides with what has been given above, except that the hand supporting the lintel in the Mahābalipuram panel is here shown as offering protection. Tumburu is also seen above on the floral arch, flying in the air.

The exact form of Vāmana, prior to his manifestation as Trivikrama, is, according to Hēmādri, that of a fat young student of the Vēdas with crooked joints, holding a staff in his hand and wearing on his back the skin of a black buck *(krishnājina)* (fig. 22). Representations of Vāmana figures with water-pot in one hand and an umbrella in the other[2] on demarcation stones of fields granted in charity, were quite common even down to the end of the nineteenth century. This auspicious figure evidently denoted fortune and was appropriately connected with boundary stones and the measurement of land. A festival in honour of Bali is still observed by the people of Mysore on the first day after the Dīpāvali-*Amāvāsyā*. In Malabar people connect Bali with

[1] Evidently Tumburu with drum in hand, leading the hosts of gods. Mr. Venkayya takes the same figure in the Nāmakkal rock-cut temples to be Jāmbavat; see Madras Epigraphical Report for 1906, p. 76.

[2] This is the description of Vāmana as given in the *Pāncharātrāgama*.

FIG. 21.—Trivikrama ; Kumbakōnam.

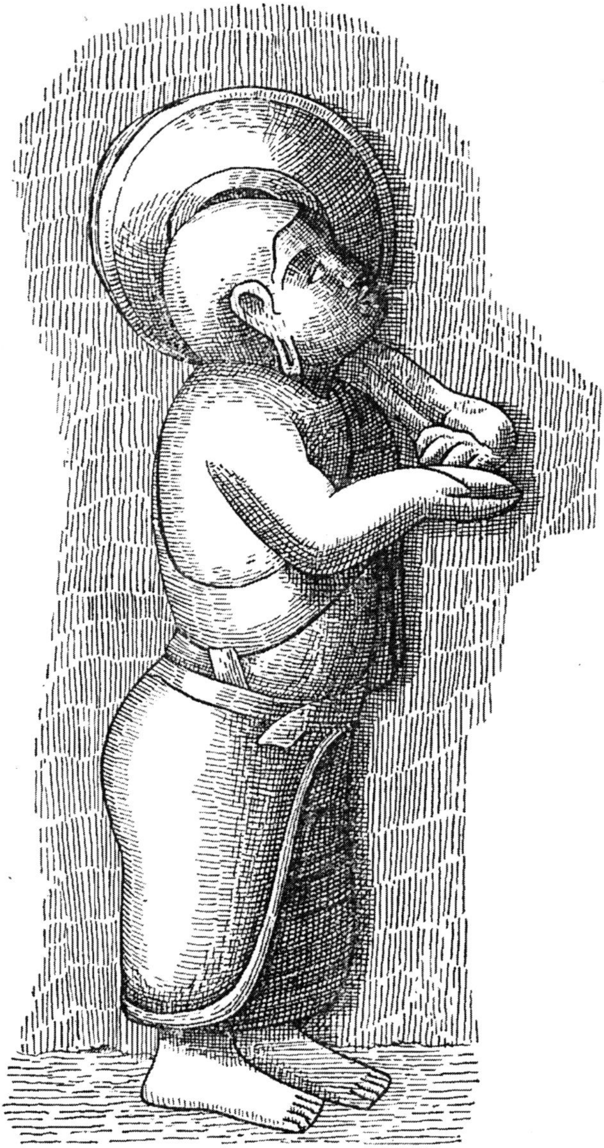

FIG. 22.—Vâmana ; Nâmakkal.

their national harvest festival, the Ōnam, in which they worship a clay figure of this high-minded emperor. It is supposed that the king is permitted by Vishnu to visit every year the fair earth over which he once ruled and to satisfy himself that the people are quite as happy and glad as in his time.

VI

RĀMA incarnation.

We now come to the *avatār* of Rāma, Rāmachandra or Rāmabhadra, the hero of the beautiful epic *Rāmāyana*, which in its various aspects has permeated the life of the Indian people and moulded their character to a great extent. Rāma was the eldest son of Dasaratha, the king of Ayōdhyā (Oudh). As such, his images do not, like those of the *avatārs* so far described,—*avatārs* which were sudden outbursts of divine energy—exhibit either the four arms of the gods or the distinguishing Vaishnavite symbols of conch, discus, club and lotus. Human in form, but god in essence, Rāma is always represented as a royal personage of bewitching beauty, well developed in body, having broad eyes, long arms, curly tresses, ornaments and auspicious marks that indicate high birth and noble character. Paintings of Rāma's life are numerous and cover the whole period of his history from his birth to his passing away bodily from this world into the depths of the Sarayū river. In many South-Indian temples may be observed scenes from the *Rāmāyana*, either painted on the walls or cut into panels, forming continuous belts round the central shrine or the *prākāra* wall.[1] When represented as the consecrated deity within a temple, Rāma is generally seen to be a standing figure with his queen Sītā on the left and his faithful brother Lakshmana on the right. He and his brother hold bows and arrows. The bow is called *kōdanda* and so Rāma with the bow is sometimes known as Kōdanda-Rāma.

In the accompanying illustration of metallic images from Rāmēsvaram (fig. 23) the positions of Sītā and Lakshmana are interchanged and the arrows and quivers are missing. The two images at either extreme represent their faithful servant Hanumān (see below p. 64). As stated in the *Silpasangraha*, the figures of Rāma are distinguished as independent and dependent. In the former case he stands alone and has four arms, two of which hold the bow and the arrow and the other two, the conch and the discus. In the latter he has two arms and may be accompanied by his three brothers, his queen

[1] For example, in the Hazāra-Rāmasvāmin temple at Hampi; in the Rāmasvāmin temple at Kumbakōnam; and in the Tennapuram temple at Chandragiri, Chittoor district.

FIG. 23.—Rama and group (metal); Râmesvaram.

Sītā, the monkey hosts and the Rākshasa chiefs headed by Vibhīshana. Rāma with Sītā on his side is generally contemplated upon as seated in the aerial car *Pushpaka* in the *virāsana* posture within a golden pavilion and underneath the celestial tree *(kalpa-vriksha)*. In his front stands Hanumān reading, while Rāma is explaining the mystery of philosophy to the crowds of sages who gather round him along with his royal brothers Bharata, Lakshmana and Satrughna.[1]

VII

Krishna is the next *avatār* of Vishnu[2] which is highly venerated by the Hindus. The Bhāgavata-*Purāna* which describes in detail the early life of Krishna in Brindāvana (Brindāban) has provided more material for iconology than his subsequent career as the moving spirit of the *Mahābhārata*-war, the author of the "Divine Song" *Bhagavad-Gītā* or the benevolent chief of Dvārakā (Dwārka, Baroda). KRISHNA incarnation.

Three stages in the life of Krishna have been marked out to be the most prominent. As a baby, not yet weaned from his mother's breast, he is represented in the arms of Yasōdā. This form of Krishna receives the name Santāna-Gōpāla. Also as a baby divine, identified with Supreme Vishnu, he is sometimes pictured as lying on a banyan-leaf (Vatapatrasāyin) sucking the toe of his leg held by the hand. These pictures of the baby-god are commonly seen in paintings. SANTĀNA-GŌPĀLA. VATAPATRASĀYIN.

Krishna is also represented as a winsome boy, full of fun and frolic and fond of thieving milk and butter from the neighbouring cottages of cowherds living at Brindāvana. It is said that on one occasion Yasōdā punished him by tying him up to a mortar. The child then ran along, dragging the mortar behind him; but in trying to pass between two tall and stout trees standing close together, the heavy mortar was caught between and felled them down; when lo!

[1] This conception of Rāma is perhaps to be traced to the fact that in the work called *Vāsishtharāmāyana*, Rāma is stated to have given lessons in philosophy to his family priest Vasishtha. The story of the *Rāmāyana* as described by the poet Vālmīki, is said to be referred to in the Mantra of the Rig-Vēda, beginning with the words *bhadrō bhadrayā*, etc. The explanatory comment *(nirukta)* is, however, not included in Yāska's *Nirukta*. The historical development of Rāma and Krishna cults have been fully dealt with by Dr. R. G. Bhandarkar in his *Vaishnavism*, *Saivism*, etc.

[2] The verse which is usually quoted in connexion with the ten *avatārs* of Vishnu, mentions Balarāma or Haladhara "the bearer of the plough," as the incarnation which came next after the epic hero Rāma. Krishna, the younger brother of Balarāma, being, however, considered to be Vishnu himself, receives divine honours in preference to Balarāma. The famous temple at Pūri-Jagannāth contains figures of Balarāma and Krishna with their sister Subhadrā standing between them.

the trees assumed the shape of the two sons of Kubēra, the god of riches, who being cursed by the sage Nārada to assume the shape of trees had been waiting long to be thus restored by the Lord Krishna to their original form. The first part of this incident is represented in fig. 24.

In South India pictures of Krishna with a pot of butter under his left arm and eating out of a ball of it placed in the palm of his right hand are not uncommon. On either side of him are represented shepherd girls of Brindāvana.[1] This form of Krishna, though very often meditated upon and sung about even in nursery rhymes, is rarely worshipped as the chief figure in temples—a famous exception to this being Udipi in the South Canara district, where a big temple, richly endowed, is maintained for the worship of the god Bāla-

BĀLA-KRISHNA.

Krishna.[2] In the Madras Museum are two metallic images of dancing Krishna, one of which holds in its right hand a ball of butter[3] (fig. 25). A peacock's feather stuck into the tuft of hair knotted overhead is, along with the other golden jewellery peculiar to children, a special feature of Krishna as a boy. Gold and silver images of this form of Krishna in miniature are among the set of idols worshipped daily in an orthodox Brāhmana's house. Vaishnavism in its various forms prevailing throughout India praises the child form of Krishna in the sweetest of strains with an overflow of devotion peculiar to that creed alone.

KĀLIYA-KRISHNA.

Another story of the boy Krishna is represented in his dance on the head of a serpent named Kāliya (the black). Kāliya was hiding in a pond in the Yamunā river and making the whole neighbourhood poisonous to all living beings. One day the cattle tended by Krishna and his companions strayed into this region and were thereby poisoned. Krishna then plunged into the pond and holding the viper by the tail

---

[1] The name given to this figure in the *Silparatna* is Santāna-Gōpāla, already referred to. Krishna under this designation is described as a young playful baby decorated with the jewels of children, holding fresh butter in his hand and surrounded by *Gōpi*-women. He wears also a necklace with a pair of tiger's claws decorating it. A variety of this same Krishna is sometimes represented to be riding on a chariot and to have four arms in two of which are seen the Vaishnava symbols *sankha* and *chakra*.

[2] Krishnarāya, the well known Vijayanagara king of the sixteenth century A.D., is stated to have installed in the Krishnasvāmin temple near Hampi, an image of Bāla-Krishna which he had brought as a trophy from Udayagiri (Nellore district) and to have given many ornaments and villages to it.

[3] The *Brāhmiya-Silpa* refers to the dance of Krishna called *Navanita-nritta* "the butter-dance" in which the god bends his legs and dances stretching out one of his arms.

FIG. 24.—Krishna tied to a mortar ; Penukonda.

FIG. 25.—Butter-dance of Bāla-Krishṇa (metal); Madras Museum

in one hand began to dance heavily on his raised hoods. The demon writhed under the pressure of the god's tiny feet, vomiting blood profusely from each of his several mouths, and was completely exhausted and overcome. Then at last the serpent Kāliya recognized the Lord and took himself away to a remote island in the far-off sea. The esoteric sense of this is clear. The serpent represents the embodiment of all that is vile and wicked in this world; the dance of Krishna represents the fight with evil and its final conquest by the Divine Spirit. Kāliya-Krishna is found only as a decorative figure in temples but not as the object of worship in the central shrine. As in the case of Bāla-Krishna, miniature figures of Kāliya-Krishna are often found among the images of worship in a Brāhmana's house. A copper idol representing this sport of Krishna was discovered some years ago among the treasure trove found at Kāttu-Edayāru in the South Arcot district (fig. 26). The figure has two hands, a jewelled crown and the usual ornaments. Being a copper image it may be inferred that the idol was used only for processions in the temple to which it originally belonged. According to the *Silpasāra* the right foot of Kālingamardana (i.e., Kāliya-Krishna) is slightly bent and the left raised up. Of the two arms the left is stretched out in the *abhaya* posture and the right holds the tail of the serpent. The figure is fully decorated with ornaments and is dark in colour. The illustration from Kāttu-Edayāru shows the same features except that the positions of the right and left legs are interchanged.

The third and the most divine sport of Krishna is his moonlight dance on the sand-banks of the Jumna in the company of the damsels of Brindāvana. The inspired poet Līlāsuka, describing this dance, says that "there, in the circle of dancers (filled with love for Krishna) was seen between damsel and damsel a Mādhava (Krishna) and between Mādhava and Mādhava a damsel; and in the centre of the group again, was the son of Dēvakī playing upon his flute," thereby indicating in poetic language the mystic significance of the dance. Of the many *Gōpi* (cow-herd) girls thus in attendance on Krishna in his early life in Brindāvana the most beloved was Rādhā, so much so that Rādhā-Krishna is the name by which he is addressed by the most ecstatic of the zealous Vaishnava cult. RĀDHĀ-KRISHNA.

Images of the flute-playing Krishna generally called Vēnu-Gōpāla (Muralīdhara) without, however, the circle of dancers, are largely worshipped in temples. He stands on his left leg with the right bent across and resting on the toe, VĒNU-GŌPĀLA.

FIG. 26.—Serpent-dance of Kāliya-Krishna (metal); Madras Museum.

and plays upon the flute. When the figure is intended for worship in temples the two upper hands will hold the conch and the discus and there will usually also be the images of his two consorts Rukminī and Satyā on either side (fig. 27).[1] In the hundred-pillared *mandapa* of the Varadarājasvāmin temple at Little Conjeeveram is a figure of the flute-playing Krishna with ten arms (fig. 28). The *Pāncharātrāgama* calls this form of Krishna by the name Madana-Gōpāla. In paintings Vēnu-Gōpāla is often represented as leaning against a cow, with one foot bent crosswise and resting on the toe. Cows and cow-herds are also often shown gathering round him. The dance with *Gōpis*, with which the flute-playing Krishna is intimately connected, is found only in drawings. The esoteric sense of this flute-play and the dance is the supreme joy which the devotees experience in moments of overflowing love in the presence of the object of their devotion.

MADANA-GŌPĀLA.

GOVARDHANA KRISHNA

Another well-known sport of Krishna during his boyhood was the lifting up of the hill called Gōvardhana. He is said to have held the hill aloft so as to give shelter to the cow-herds of Brindāvana from a continuous down-pour of rain sent down by Indra in anger in order to flood their small village. A beautiful old representation of this scene comes from the Seven Pagodas (fig. 29) where, in the so-called Krishna-*mandapa*, Krishna stands in the centre with his left hand raised straight up to support the hill, while his right hand is held in the posture of offering boons *(varada)*.[2] All round the god are seen cows and cow-herds, men and women, the latter carrying pots of milk, butter, curds or other cooked offerings to the god, and leading their young ones by the hand or accompanying their husbands. The ornaments of Krishna in this picture are very sparing. They are the usual large ear-rings peculiar to the sculpture of the Pallava period, bracelets, armlets and the waist-band. The high crown on the head is also a noticeable feature. This representation differs, however, from the description given in the *Silpasāra* where the god is described as having one hand with flute resting on his waist and the other supporting the hill.

---

[1] At Turaiyûr in the Trichinopoly district the god worshipped in the shrine has only two hands. Hēmādri states that the image of Gōpāla playing on the flute is made with the head ornament of peacock feathers, blue body and two arms. The *Silpasangraha* adds that he is chiefly found in a standing attitude.

[2] Dr. Vogel says that the central figure of the group is Balarāma (Baladēva), the brother of Krishna (Archæological Survey Report for 1910-11, p. 51, note 1). He is seen throwing his left hand round the neck of a cow-herd boy who rests his hands crossed on the head of a long hatchet.

FIG. 27.—Vēnu-Gōpāla ; Madras Museum.

FIG. 28.—Madana-Gōpāla; Little Conjeeveram.

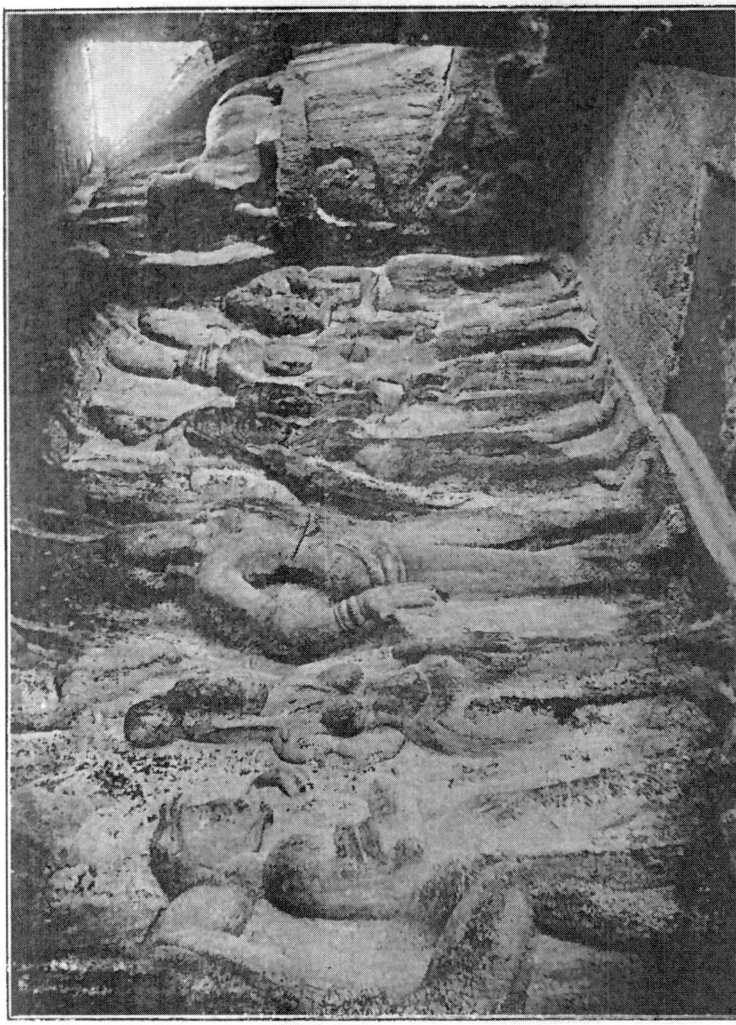

FIG. 29.—Gōvardhana-Krishna ; Seven Pagodas.

Again Krishna on the tree is a familiar figure in paintings and decorative sculptures of temples. The story is related in the Bhāgavata-*Purāna* how one day Krishna saw the cow-herd girls bathing naked in the Jumna leaving their clothes on the sand banks of the river and how he took away their clothes and got up a tree standing near by. He did not restore the clothes to the girls till they confessed their error in bathing naked against the teaching of the *Sāstras*. One of the usual processional vehicles in Vishnu temples is the *punnai*-tree with the naked *Gōpis* standing round it and begging for the return of their clothes (fig. 30). GŌPIVASTRĀPAHĀRAKA.

After leaving Brindāvana, Krishna became the clever and astute statesman and warrior of Dvārakā and took an active part in the war between Kauravas and Pāndavas described in the *Mahābhārata*. He was on the side of the Pāndavas; he was an intimate friend of Arjuna (or Pārtha) and even served him as his charioteer on the battle-field. Hence Krishna is also known by the name of Pārthasārathi, the name of the god in the famous temple at Triplicane. It was on this occasion in the battle-field, when Arjuna was dismayed at the prospect of a bloody war with his relatives, that the divine charioteer Krishna is said to have delivered to Arjuna the famous discourse known as the *Bhagavad-Gītā*. A fine illustration of the scene comes from the Kēsavasvāmin temple at Pushpagiri (fig. 31). The story runs that Arjuna and Krishna were bosom friends in far earlier ages, when under the names Nara and Nārāyana they are supposed to have performed penance in Badarikāsrama. PĀRTHASĀRATHI.

VIII

Two other *avatārs* of Vishnu, viz., Buddha and Kalki may be noticed. The latter is only a prospective incarnation in which the god is expected to appear as a powerful hero riding on horse-back, sword in hand, to suppress the growing wickedness of the Mlēchchhas. The Buddha incarnation of Vishnu is, no doubt, counted among the ten *avatārs* but is rarely found worshipped in Hindu temples.[1] Buddha is BUDDHA and KALKI incarnations.

---

[1] The *Brāhmiya-Silpa* does not include Buddha in the *avatārs* of Vishnu. It mentions Krishna in the place of Buddha. The *Mānasāra* gives a complete description of the figures of Buddha which it says must be made of white stone, very much like the images of Jina (below, p. 262f.) seated or standing on a lion-pedestal under the *pipal* or the wish-giving celestial tree, with two hands, *ushnisha* (crown) a yellow cloth, broad forehead, long ear-lobes, big eyes, high nose, smiling countenance, long arms, broad chest, fleshy limbs and body. When standing, his arms must be made to hang down loosely.

FIG. 30.—Krishna on the *punnai*-tree (wood); Kumbakōnam.

FIG. 31.—Pârthasârathi teaching the *Bhagavad-Gîtâ* to Arjuna ; Pushpagiri.

regarded by some as an *avatār* designed to lead the *asuras* into ruin by giving them bad advice. Others like Jayadēva regard him rightly as an incarnation of mercy who came to teach the people the essential cruelty of animal sacrifices.

IX

Other forms of Vishnu not included in the *avatārs*. ANANTAŚĀYIN, PADMANĀBHA or RANGANĀTHA.

Besides the *avatārs* mentioned above, there are other forms of Vishnu which are also often found in South-Indian temples. The most important of such is his reclining form, known by the names Anantasāyin (or Sēshasāyin), Padmanābha and Ranganātha.[1] The temples at Srīrangam and Trivandrum may be specially mentioned as the places where this form of Vishnu is worshipped. In Tamil he is known as Palligondān. A good illustration (fig. 32) comes from the old sculptures at Mahābalipuram. In the so-called Mahishāsura-*mandapa*, on the proper right wall of the front verandah is depicted the scene under reference. Here on the coils of the serpent Ananta sleeps on his back a gigantic figure of Vishnu with two arms. The right hand is carelessly thrown on the body of the serpent while the left hand is raised up at the elbow. The god wears a cloth round the waist, which reaches down to the feet. The usual *udarabandhana* is also tied round the lower part of the stomach in the form of a girdle, its ends gracefully hanging down and touching the right side of the serpent couch. The garland round the neck (i.e., the *vanamālā*) has slipped down the right arm of the god, thus emphasizing his sleeping posture. By the side of the serpent couch, near the feet of Vishnu, is the figure of Lakshmī kneeling down and worshipping him with folded hands. In front of her are two other figures also seated by the side of the serpent couch. These may be the two colleagues of Vishnu, viz., Brahmā and Siva, or the attendants Jaya and Vijaya. Above the sleeping god in the air are two flying figures, one a female and the other a fat figure, probably a goblin. Beyond his feet and looking him straight in the face are two stalwart figures standing one in a defiant attitude with a club in his hand and the other dissuading him from what looks apparently like a murderous attack on the god. The Padma-*Purāna* gives a

[1] The *Mayamata* says that the serpent, the couch of Anantasayanā, may be of five or seven hoods, its white colour indicating great bliss. Padmanābha means "he of the lotus-navel"; and we see, in figures of Anantasayana, the navel of the god sending forth a stock at the end of which is a lotus flower and in it the four-faced Brahmā. Ranganātha is "the lord of the *ranga*, the assembly-hall." It might be noted that in the illustrations of Anantasayana the central figure of Vishnu is surrounded by all the other gods as if in an assembly-hall.

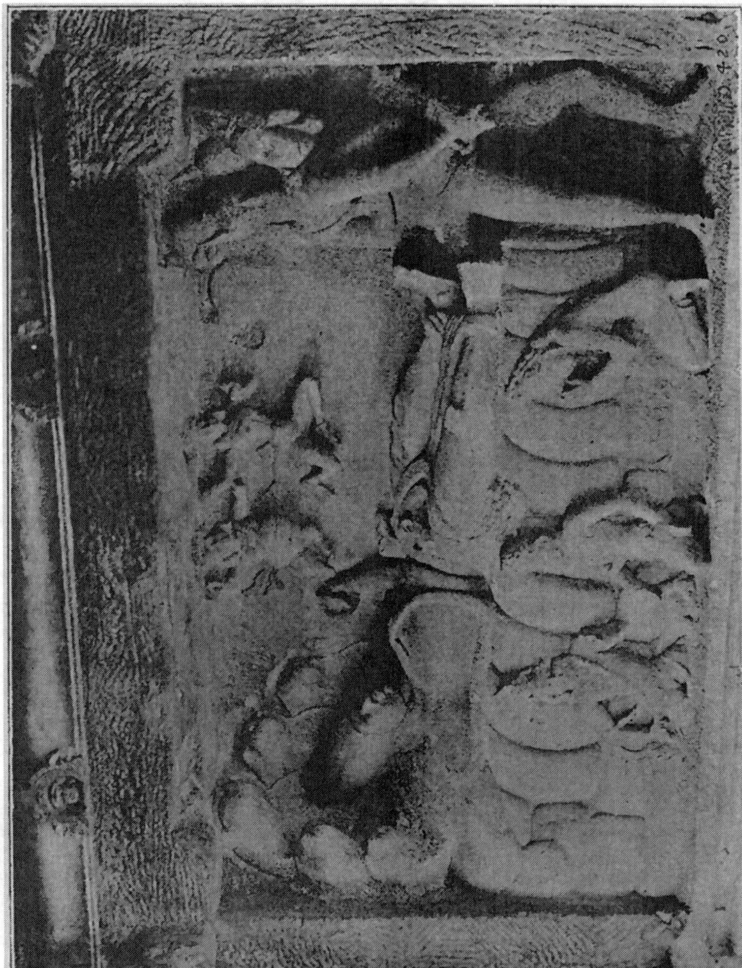

FIG. 32.—Anantasāyin ; Seven Pagodas.

description of Vishnu, which comes very near to what has been depicted above. It says: "The god of gods sleeps on the serpent. One of his legs lies on the thigh of Lakshmī, while the other is placed on the body of the serpent. He has two hands, one of which is stretched along the right thigh and the other is placed over his head. Brahmā is comfortably seated on the lotus which springs from the navel of Vishnu. Entangled in the stem of the lotus stand the demons Madhu and Kaitabha. The symbols of the god, viz., the conch, discus, club and lotus are all represented about him, each assuming a body."[1] A similar description is given by Hēmādri under the term Jalasayana.

JALASAYANA.

VAIKUNTHA-NĀRĀYANA.

God Vishnu seated comfortably on the serpent couch is named Vaikuntha-Nārāyana[2] (fig. 33). The left leg is stretched down and the right is bent at the knee; the left hand rests on the knee-joint, while the right hand rests carelessly thrown back on the head of the serpent; the two back hands hold the weapons *sankha* and *chakra*. The image is decorated with jewels and by its side are his consorts Lakshmī and Prithvī.

LAKSHMĪ-NĀRĀYANA.

Lakshmī-Nārāyana is another of Vishnu's seated forms where, to the left of the god, by his side or sometimes on his thigh, is found seated the image of Lakshmī throwing her right hand round the neck of the god while she holds in her left a lotus. The left hand of Vishnu similarly passes round the waist of Lakshmī. A female deity called Siddhi stands near, with a fly-whisk in her hand. The vehicle Garuda is on the right side at the foot of the god. The *sankha* and *chakra* not being held by the god are carried by two dwarf male figures standing in front of him; Brahmā and Siva also stand by, worshipping Vishnu with folded hands[3] (fig. 34).

---

[1] Vāsudēva described by Hēmādri as a standing Vishnu figure of four arms, holds in the two upper hands the lotus and the conch and instead of having in the two lower, the weapons *chakra* (discus) and *gadā* (club), he places the palms of these hands on the heads of two dwarf figures, one male and one female, holding *chauris* in their hands and looking at the face of the god These dwarf figures are stated to be the personified weapons *chakra* and *gadā*; (see *Mayūrabhanja*, fig. 16, on plate facing p. xl). The descriptions given by the same author of Sankarshana, Pradyumna and Aniruddha—other standing forms of Vishnn—refer also to personified weapons.

[2] See the Madras Epigraphical Report for 1906, p. 76. The *Brāhmiya-Silpa* calls this same figure Ādimūrti and describes him as being attended by gods and *rishis* in a worshipping attitude.

[3] Hēmādri. According to the *Silpasangraha*, Lakshmī-Nārāyana has four arms in which he displays the conch and the discus and the protecting and the boon-giving postures. Mr. Rea portrays a fine picture of Lakshmī-Nārāyana from Nīlagunda (Bellary district) on Plate LIII of his *Chalukyan Architecture*.

FIG. 33.—Vaikuntha-Nārāyana ; Nāmakkal.

FIG. 34.—Lakshmī-Nārāyana ; Nāmakkal.

The *Silpasāra* mentions an image called Garuda-Nārāyana wherein Vishnu is seen riding on Garuda, holding a bow and arrow, conch and discus. An illustration from Chidambaram (fig. 35), which is mutilated, is apparently one of Garuda-Nārāyāna. On a pillar in the Rāmasvāmin temple at Kumbakōnam is a fine representation of this form of Vishnu in the attitude of blessing the elephant *(gajēndra)* after rescuing it from the attack of a crocodile. The scene is generally known as Gajēndra-mōksha (fig. 36). GARUDA-NĀRĀYANA. GAJĒNDRA-MŌKSHA.

Figures of Vishnu, with four arms seated in a meditative posture, are probably those of Yōgēsvara-Vishnu, described by Ḥēmādri as seated on a lotus, with eyes half-closed and directed towards the tip of the nose. An image (fig. 37) from the ruined Vishnu temple at Hūvinahadagalli (Bellary district) illustrates this form. Another image, probably of this same form of Vishnu but seated on the serpent couch, comes from Kumbakōnam (fig. 38). Here the god is bathed by two goddesses with pots in their hands. YŌGĒSVARA-VISHNU.

The twenty-four well-known names of Vishnu repeated by the Brāhmanas in their daily prayer known as *sandhyāvandana*, are represented each by a standing figure of the god with four hands holding the four symbols *sankha* (conch), *chakra* (discus), *gadā* (club) and *padma* (lotus), in different combinations. Consequently we may often find in Vishnu temples images named Trivikrama, Vāmana, Padmanābha, Narasimha or Krishna represented as plain standing figures of Vishnu, without reference to any of the *Purānic* scenes connected with these gods. Four of the above mentioned twenty-four forms, viz., Vāsudēva, Sankarshana, Pradyumna and Aniruddha are sometimes represented by different weapons. Twenty-four general forms of standing Vishnu.

The two illustrations in the accompanying plates (figs. 39 and 40) show another form of standing Vishnu, known as Pānduranga or Vithōba. The characteristic feature of the image is that it has two arms which, being bent at the elbow, are placed on its hips. A poem in praise of this form of Vishnu, entitled *Pāndurangāshtaka*, is attributed to Sankarāchārya of about the eighth century A.D. PĀNDURANGA or VITHŌBA.

Hayagrīva is still another form of standing Vishnu, represented with the head of a horse. Hēmādri describes him as having a white complexion, and placing his feet on the hands of the goddess Earth. He has eight hands, in four of which are held the Vaishnavite symbols conch, discus, club and lotus. With the others he carries the four Vēdas personified. The *Pāncharātrāgama* mentions only four hands in which are seen the conch, rosary, book and the *jnāna-mudrā*. HAYAGRĪVA.

FIG. 35.—Garuda-Nārāyana ; Chidambaram.

FIG. 36.—Garuda-Nārāyana and Gajēndra-mōksha ; Kumbakōnam.

FIG. 37.—Yōgēsvara-Vishnu ; Hūvinahadagalli.

FIG. 38.—Yōgēsvara-Vishnu (?) ; Kumbakōnam.

FIG. 39.— Pânduranga ; Tirupati.

FIG. 40.—Pāndurañga ; Ahōbalam.

VENKATĒSA. Venkatēsa or Venkataramana (also called Srīnivāsa) is a name of Vishnu applied to the god on the Tirupati Hill. He is in form like one of the twenty-four images of Vishnu described above.[1]

X

PRADYUMNA, KĀMADĒVA OR MANMATHA. Pradyumna, which is mentioned among the twenty-four general names of Vishnu, occurs in the Sanskrit lexicon *Amarakōsa* as a synonym of the god Kāmadēva or Manmatha, who is recognized as a son of Krishna-Vishnu. His consort is 'Love' (Rati). This god of Love was reduced to ashes by Siva. His form that was thus destroyed is still alive but is visible only to Rati. The metaphysical meaning of the story is more or less clear. Rati and Manmatha are often found among the sculptures in a temple. The latter is represented as a graceful youth of unparalleled elegance. He has eight hands in four of which he holds the conch, lotus, bow and arrow. The four other arms embrace his four beautiful wives called Rati (love), Prīti (pleasure), Sakti (power) and Bhēda-Sakti (jealousy). Kāma has five arrows, each arrow being a fragrant flower; the crocodile *(makara)* is his banner. More often he is represented with two hands, riding on a chariot (or a parrot) with his chief queen Rati by his side (fig. 41). Vasanta, the Spring, is his intimate friend and ally. His five arrows are the flowers of lotus, *asōka*, mango, jasmine, and blue-lily; and he shoots them with his graceful bow of sugarcane. *Mayamata* says that Manmatha's arrows are made of the cruel teeth of women and are called *tāpani*, "the tormentor," *dāhini* "the consumer," *sarvamōhini* "that which completely infatuates," *visva-mardini* "the all-destroyer" and *mārani* "the killer."

XI

VISHVAKSĒNA. Vishvaksēna, a synonym for Vishnu also found in the lexicon *Amarakōsa*, is recognized as a Vaishnava god who, like Ganēsa of the Saivas (described below), is worshipped by the Srī-Vaishnavas, at the beginning of every ceremony in order to avoid obstacles. He has his face turned towards the south and is a guardian deity in Vishnu temples. In three of his hands he holds the usual Vaishnavite symbols, viz., the conch,

---

[1] It is believed, and perhaps on reasonable grounds, that the image on the Tirupati Hill is a combined form of Vishnu and Siva. The name Vrisha-saila, i.e., "Bull-hill" applied to the mountain on which the temple is situated, indicates also the Saiva nature of the god. In later times, the name Sēsha-saila "the hill of the serpent god Sēsha" came to be applied to it.

FIG. 41.—Rati-Manmatha; Chidambaram.

discus and the club and in the fourth exhibits the threatening finger-pose called *tarjani*. He is seated with his right leg hanging down from the pedestal and the left bent crosswise and placed on the same [fig. 160 (*c*), below].

GARUDA. Vishnu's vehicle Garuda is installed in every Vaishnavite temple right opposite to the central shrine and is a standing human figure of stone or mortar, with a beak-shaped nose and with spreading wings proceeding from his back on either side. He has his two arms folded over the breast in a worshipping posture (fig. 42).[1] When made into a processional image of metal, Garuda is represented as kneeling on the left knee, the right foot being firmly placed on the ground and a serpent decorating his head.[2]

XII

HANUMĀN. Hanumān, the monkey-god, has been already referred to as a great devotee of Vishnu intimately connected with the incarnation Rāma-*avatār*. In Southern India he is very popular, even insignificant villages containing a shrine for Hanumān. He is represented in two postures.[3] When included in the group of Rāma, Lakshmana and Sītā, he stands at a distance on one side, or opposite to them, in a humble and devotional attitude, with the two hands folded together, the tail hanging down close to his feet.[4] In shrines exclusively

---

[1] According to the *Silparatna*, Garuda figures may also be shown with the two hands pointing the *abhaya* and the *varada* postures. Occasionally, Garuda may be made to carry in his right hand a pot of nectar. This is evidently a reference to the story that Garuda while young carried away from Indra the pot of nectar, in order to fulfil his mother's promise to Kadru, the mother of serpents.

[2] The *Silpasangraha* describes a form of Garuda who has fierce protruding teeth and eight arms in six of which he has the conch, discus, club, lotus and the nectar-pot while the others are stretched out to receive the feet of the Lord (Vishnu). It is further stated that the eight lords of serpents are worn as jewels by him, thus showing that Garuda had completely subdued the Nāgas. Garuda when represented with four arms is called Vainatēya. It may be noted that the bird Garuda is of Vēdic fame, his body being supposed to be completely made up of the Vēdas. A Vēdic sacrifice called Garuda-chayana is performed by offering oblations to the gods on a platform built in the shape of Garuda. Vishnu is sometimes known as Yajna-purusha—the personified god of sacrifice.

[3] The *Silparatna* mentions a third posture in which Hanumān is described as a *yōgin*, teaching philosophy to a number of pupils who surround him.

[4] See above, fig. 23. Here, at the right end of the picture Hanumān is seen in a submissive attitude while another figure of his at the left end, carries in both hands two Siva-*lingas* which Rāma had ordered him to bring for establishing at Rāmēsvaram, on his way back from Lankā. *Visvakarma*, Part VI, Plate 100, also gives a metallic figure of Hanumān from Ceylon, with his hands stretched out, indicating evidently a mixed feeling of wonder and despair.

FIG. 42.—Garuda ; Tanjore.

dedicated to him he is always the heroic Hanumān, who, on seeing his beloved masters Rāma and Lakshmana faint with fatigue on the battle field of Lankā, flew in an amazingly short time to the Himalayas and, uprooting a whole hill containing drugs that have power to raise a dead man to life, returned to revive Rāma and Lakshmana and with them also the millions of dead monkeys. His heroism, strength and devotion are always admired and the one aim of sculptors in cutting a figure of Hanumān is to give effect to these three special characteristics. No wonder that even the Muhammadans (or, rather Muhammadan converts of later ages) who set high value on physical strength and individual heroism came to appreciate the story of Hanumān and to erect shrines for him. There is inscriptional evidence to prove that in the Ceded districts, where the Muhammadan influence has been very strong, certain classes of Mussalmans are still devoted to this heroic servant of Rāma. This must also have been the object of Chiefs in erecting shrines for Hanumān at the gates of their forts, viz., to infuse into the hearts of their fighting men the spirit of loyal attachment to their masters and indomitable heroism. Sometimes Hanumān may also be represented with hands showing the *abhaya* and the *varada* postures.

XIII

SUDARSANA. Of the Vaishnava symbols and weapons referred to in the previous paragraphs as being sometimes personified, the discus *(chakra)* under the name Sudarsana deserves special mention, it being separately worshipped in the Srī-Vaishnava temples under the name Chakra-Perumāl (figs. 43 and 44). The *Silpasāra* describes Sudarsana to be brilliant as fire, with sixteen arms holding the weapons conch, discus, bow, axe, sword, arrow, trident, noose, goad, lotus, thunderbolt, shield, plough, pestle, club and spear. The figure has protruding teeth, fiery hair and three eyes. It is fully decorated and stands in front of a *shatkōna* or hexagon. Dancing thus amidst the flames of the discus, the Sudarsana is supposed to kill all enemies. Sometimes the image may be represented with eight or four arms holding the discus in all of them.

Mr. Longhurst has supplied two other photographs (fig. 45) in the first of which Sudarsana appears to be similar in all details to the Tirupati figure No. 43, but has at the back of it an equilateral triangle within which is the seated figure of Nrisimha in the *yogāsana* attitude (see above, fig. 19) with flames of fire proceeding from his crown. This form of Nrisimha is

FIG. 43.—Sudarsana ; Tirupati.

FIG. 44.—Sudarsana, back view ; Tirupati.

FIG. 45.—Sudarsana, front and back view (metal); Dādikkombu.

evidently what is popularly known as Jvālā-Nrisimha "the fiery Nrisimha." It may be noted that the famous Chakrapāni temple at Kumbakōnam is dedicated to the discus Sudarsana of Vishnu.

XIV.

Sāligrāma stones.

Apart from the various forms of Vishnu detailed above, every Hindu worships certain formless stones, called Sāligrāma, as these more satisfactorily answer to the idea of the formless Brahman. The Sāligrāma stones are generally picked up from the bed of the river Gandakī (in North Bihar) or are made of a particular kind of stone procurable at Dvārakā. The former are perfectly smooth and rounded pebbles and are heavier than ordinary stones. The belief is that within them is found gold or other heavy metal. The Sāligrāma stones are believed to possess certain mystic and sacred virtues. In the country of Avantī, at the foot of the sacred hill known as Hariparvata, is stated to be a big pond called Chakratīrtha, from which flows the river Gandakī. On rare and auspicious occasions, within this pond, are produced the Sāligrāma stones, which, after remaining for 1,000 years in water, become the abode of Vishnu, who then assuming the form of a brilliant little insect called *vajrakita* enters into them and bores a hole with his mouth, forming therein a discus *(chakra)* of numerous varieties. The stones are of many colours and sizes and are distinguished by these *chakras* to represent either Vāsudēva (white colour), Hiranyagarbha (blue), Pradyumna (red), Vishnu (black), Srī-Nārāyana (dark-green), Narasimha (tawny), or Vāmana (deep-blue). Eighty-nine varieties are recognized, each bearing a different name of Vishnu. One well-known test of their suitability for worship consists in placing them in milk or in rice, when, a genuine Sāligrāma is supposed to increase in size and in weight. A strange feature about these stones is that, while they mostly represent the forms of Vishnu, some are stated to be also forms of Siva, Sakti, Sūrya (Sun), Ganapati and the Planets. The Sāligrāmas are never fixed on pedestals as the *lingas* of Siva (see below, p. 72) or as the images of other gods. In many of the South-Indian temples of Vishnu, garlands of Sāligrāma stones are hung round the necks of images. Sāligrāma forms the most important object of daily worship in every orthodox Brāhmana's house in Southern India. The water poured over it is most holy and like the Ganges water which Brāhmanas generally preserve in their homes in sealed vessels, is offered to the dying man in order that his soul may become pure and depart in peace. The gift of Sāligrāma stones to Brāhmanas is considered one of the most meritorious acts and is as highly prized as the presentation of gold itself. Strictly religious people never sell or purchase Sāligrāmas but only acquire them by gift or by transfer. Of the sectarian Vaishnavas of the South, viz., the Srī-Vaishnavas and the Mādhvas, the latter show greater respect to the Sāligrāma stones than even for sculptured images of Vishnu.

CHAPTER IV.

SIVA.

I

Siva temples.

Siva is the third member of the Hindu Triad and in Southern India is more widely worshipped than Vishnu. Hundreds of Siva temples of historic fame are found in Southern India, round which are centred traditions of Saiva saints whose period may be assigned roughly to the seventh century A.D. One noticeable peculiarity of these ancient Siva temples is that they enshrine within them images of Vishnu as also of various other gods of the Hindu Pantheon, whereas Vishnu temples are exclusive in this respect. Exception must, however, be made in the case of some very old Vishnu temples[1] sung in the hymns of the *Nālāyiraprabandham* which are as ancient as the corresponding Saiva scriptures collectively called *Dēvāram*. Here we find Siva and Vishnu often mentioned together as located in the same temple and, in a higher philosophical sense, as forming different aspects of one and the same Divine Energy.

II

Siva-*linga*.

Siva is generally worshipped in the form of the phallus *(linga)* fixed on a pedestal. The phallic cult has been traced to very ancient times, its origin, however, being still involved in mystery. The worship of the creative energy of God, interpreted by the sense-perception of man and represented by the symbols *yōni* and *linga* in union, has apparently been as old as man himself. Whatever may be the origin of *linga*-worship, there is no doubt that it has come to be recognized like the Vaishnavite Sāligrāma described above, a perfect symbol of the formless, all-pervading Divine Being, unlimited by time and space. The Skānda-*Purāna* says:—"The sky is the shaft and the earth its pedestal; all gods dwell in the *linga;*

[1] E.g. Tirumala and Kadalmallai.

since the whole creation finds its origin and rest there, it receives the name *linga*."[1] In the introduction to his translation of the Vishnu-*Purāna* (p. lxix) Professor H. H. Wilson makes the following remarks on the *linga*-worship in India: "The *linga* is twofold, external and internal. The ignorant who need a visible sign, worship Siva through a 'mark' or 'type' which is the proper meaning of the word *linga*—of wood or stone; but the wise look upon this outward emblem as nothing and contemplate in their minds the invisible inscrutable type which is Siva himself. Whatever may have been the origin of this form of worship in India, the notions upon which it was founded according to the impure fancies of European writers are not to be traced even in the Saiva Purānas." Mr. Havell thinks that it "was in all probability originally derived from the votive *stūpa* of Buddhism."[2] If Saivism is, however, granted to be older in its origin than Buddhism—the Sākyas themselves among whom Buddha was born being mentioned as having Siva for their tutelar deity[3]—this theory cannot be upheld. Various forms of the *linga* are worshipped, from the crude uncut conical gneiss usually believed to be *svayambhū* or self-born[4] to the highly polished and hand-made shaft of 8, 16, 32 or more facets of the Pallava period.

Lingas, whether self-born or artificial are equally venerated, the latter being associated as regards their origin with the Sun, Moon, the Lords of the quarters or ancient sages of bygone millenniums. The *linga* is generally fixed in a circular or quadrangular receptacle on a high monolithic pedestal known as *yōni*, *pānivattam* or *āvadaiyār*.

It is a common adage that Siva is as fond of bathing as Vishnu is fond of decoration and the surface of the pedestal which receives the *linga* is so fashioned as to drain off the large quantity of water[5] poured over the god every day from a copper vessel with a hole at its bottom, hung directly

[1] In *Sivarahasya*, a chapter of *Saura-samhitā*, it is stated that the *linga* has a fivefold significance and denotes the primeval energy of the Creator. At the end of the creation all gods find their resting place in the *linga*,—Brahmā being absorbed into the right, Janārdana (Vishnu) into the left and Gāyatrī into the heart.

[2] *Ideals of Indian Art*, p. 87.

[3] See *Epigraphia Indica*, Vol. V, p. 3.

[4] The *Silparatna* describes this to be a long or short shaft of shattered appearance, flat like a board and many cornered with crooked horns. Bāna is another kind of *linga* which is shaped by nature and not by the chisel.

[5] According to the *Mayamata* all kinds of pedestals, whatever may be their pattern, must have a duct on their left side to carry off the surface water. These ducts are to be well decorated.

over the shaft. In a *linga* considered as a symbol of Brahman, the quadrangular bottom of the shaft is believed to represent Brahmā, the octagonal middle Vishnu and the circular upper portion Siva.[1] Sometimes a single *linga* is

Sahasra-*linga*.

known by the name Sahasra ("the thousand")-*linga* (fig. 46). It is divided into twenty-five facets, each of these latter having miniature representations of forty *lingas* and making up thus the number one thousand.

III

Round the *sanctum* of a Siva temple, on its outer wall, are usually enshrined in specially formed niches the images of Gaṇapati and Dakshināmūrti on the south, Lingōdbhava (or sometimes, Vishnu) on the west, and Brahmā and Durgā on the north. In the enclosing verandah round the central shrine may be installed the images of the sixty-three Saiva Saints, *lingas* which devout adherents might choose to establish for the merit of themselves or of their ancestors, the nine Planets *(Navagrahas)*, which, since the time astrology was established in India, have been receiving divine homage, and a host of other gods and goddesses such as Kumāra (Skanda), Vīrabhadra, Bhairava, etc. Naṭarāja or Sabhāpati "the lord of the divine congregation" is placed in a separate shrine, generally the *Sabhā-mandapa* or "the assembly hall." The goddess Pārvatī, the consort of Siva, who receives all kinds of fanciful names and surnames according to local traditions, is also enshrined separately. Sometimes it is found that every important subordinate deity has a separate shrine for itself, smaller, of course, in size than the *sanctum*.

It may be noted that, while worship is offered in the central shrine of a Siva temple only to the formless stone *linga*, for processional purposes images made of metal are used; and these are of various forms and go by various names, such as Sōmāskanda, Vrishārūdha, Gangādhara, Kalyānasundara, Ardhanāri, Bhikshāṭana, Naṭarāja, etc. Instances are not uncommon where images of Siva in one of his processional forms receives more attention from the worshippers than the *linga* itself. In Chidambaram, for example, the image of Naṭarāja receives more attention and

---

[1] The *sirōvartana* or the shaping of the top of the *linga* which, according to the *Silparatna*, may be cucumber-like, umbrella-like, crescent-like, egg-like or bubble-like, distinguishes the four different *lingas* worshipped by the four castes. The same work sets down that images may also be carved on the *linga*. Superior *lingas* are stated to vary from 7 to 9 cubits in height. Fixed *lingas* are worshipped in temples and movable *lingas* in houses.

FIG. 46.—Sahasra-*linga* ; Tiruvottiyūr.

is more famous than the movable *linga* of pebble which is known as Ratnasabhāpati, or the stone *linga* of Mūlasthāna. At Bhikshāndārkōyil in the Trichinopoly district the mendicant form of Siva is worshipped. Ardhanāri is the god worshipped at Tiruchchengōdu (Salem) and so is the bronze image of Somāskanda (under the name Tyāgarāja) worshipped at Tiruvārūr.

IV

RUDRA-MŪRTI.

Before describing some of the popular Siva-images[1] it may be useful to give a general description of Siva when he is represented in the form of an image. The common name then applied to him is Rudramūrti.[2] He has four hands, of which the two upper ones hold the *dhakkā* (kettle-drum) and the deer, the two lower hands showing the *abhaya* and the *varada* postures. His matted hair is made up in the form of a crown *(jatāmakuta)* on whose left shines the crescent of the moon and whose right is decorated with the jewel known as *arka-pushpa*. The face of a woman (i.e., of the goddess Gangā representing the river Ganges) appears over the matted hair, on the right side. He has three eyes, which represent the Sun, Moon and Fire, the last being on the forehead. He is clothed with a tiger skin above his knees and wears an undergarment and a scarf and the usual ornaments, necklace and torque, girdle round the waist, wristlets, waist-zone, armlets, arm-rings, finger-rings set with gems, anklets, and the sacred thread. The left ear of the god wears a woman's ornament called *lamba-patra*, while the right wears a man's ornament called *makara-kundala*. The left side of the neck is marked with the blue scar (caused by his having swallowed the poison *kālakūta*[3]). This general form of Siva may be represented either standing or seated on the lotus-pedestal with an aureola, and with or without his consort Pārvatī on the left side. The pedestal may also sometimes be the *mahā-pītha*, when, instead of the aureola behind the image, there may be the celestial tree *(kalpa-vriksha)*.

---

[1] Sixteen of these are mentioned in the *Silpasāra*. They are :– Sukhāsana, Vaivāhika, Umāsahita (according to the *Mayamata* Umāskanda), Vrishārūdha, Tripurāntaka or Purāri, Natarāja, Chandrasēkhara, Ardhanāri, Harihara, Chandēsvara (*Mayamata* gives Chandēsānugraha), Kāmāri, Kālanāsa, Dakshināmūrti, Bhikshātana, Sadāsiva (*Mayamata* gives Mukhalinga) and Lingōdbhava. The *Kāranāgama* mentions twenty-five.

[2] Hēmādri describes Rudra as riding on a bull and having five faces all of which are mild-looking, except the one on the right side of the central face. He has ten arms and wears garlands of skulls.

[3] See below, p. 137 f., under Srīkantha.

ASHTAMŪRTI and ĒKĀDASA-RUDRAS.

Standing images of Siva generally belong to the class known as Ashtamūrtis or Ēkādasa-Rudras. The former have generally four hands and three eyes and wear the *jatāmakuta*. The fore-arms exhibit the protecting and the boon-giving postures; while the hind arms hold the *tanka* and the antelope. The Ēkādasa-Rudras are almost similar to Rudramūrti in form, with the black scar on the neck, the crescent on the head and the scarf of tiger-skin. In place of the *dhakkā* in the right upper hand is seen the axe *(parasu)*. A form of Siva combining five bodies in one is known as Panchadēhamūrti. Though not found in any of the temples examined so far, it is often mentioned in the Tanjore inscriptions as having been installed in the Rājarājēsvara (i.e., the modern Brihadīsvara) temple by the Chōla king Rājarāja or his subordinates, in the first quarter of the eleventh century A.D. The Panchadēhamūrti consisted of five images, four of which stood in the four directions and the fifth was placed in the middle, its head being higher in level than the others.[2] One of these was called Aghōra. The *linga* with five faces called Panchamukha-*linga* is only the five-bodied Panchadēhamūrti translated in terms of the symbolical phallus.[3] It has the heads of four Siva-images figured on its four sides. The illustration from Tiruvānaikkāval (fig. 47) does not show any face at the top. The Skānda-*Purāna* mentions a seated form of Siva called Mahākailāsa or Mahā-Sadāsiva which is represented with twenty-five faces and fifty hands, wears a garland of skulls and is clothed in tiger's skin.

PANCHADĒHAMŪRTI.

MAHĀKAILĀSA OR MAHĀ-SADĀSIVA.

V.

NATARĀJA OR SABHAPATI.

Images answering to the two names Natarāja and Sabhāpati, in the Hindu Pantheon, are identical in design. Natarāja (the prince of dancers) is the well-known dancing form of god Siva. It has four arms and a body besmeared with ashes. The back arm on the right side holds the kettle-drum (*udukkai*, as it is called in Tamil) while the other presents the raised palm of protection *(abhaya)*. Of the pair on the left, the upper holds a fire-pot and the lower is bent round

---

[1] According to Hēmādri these may be substituted by the club and the trident.

[2] Jaina images called *Chaturmukha* or *Chaumukhi* are often made of a single stone. The four identical images on the four sides are surmounted by a series of umbrellas common to all, which appear like the spire of a temple (see *Epigraphia Indica*, Vol. X, p. 115). The Buddhists also seem to have possessed such figures; see Nagendra Natha Vasu's *Mayūrabhanja*, p. 41.

[3] A *linga* placed at the entrance into an old Siva temple at Raichūr (Hyderabad State) shows a combination of five *lingas*, four on the sides and one at the top.

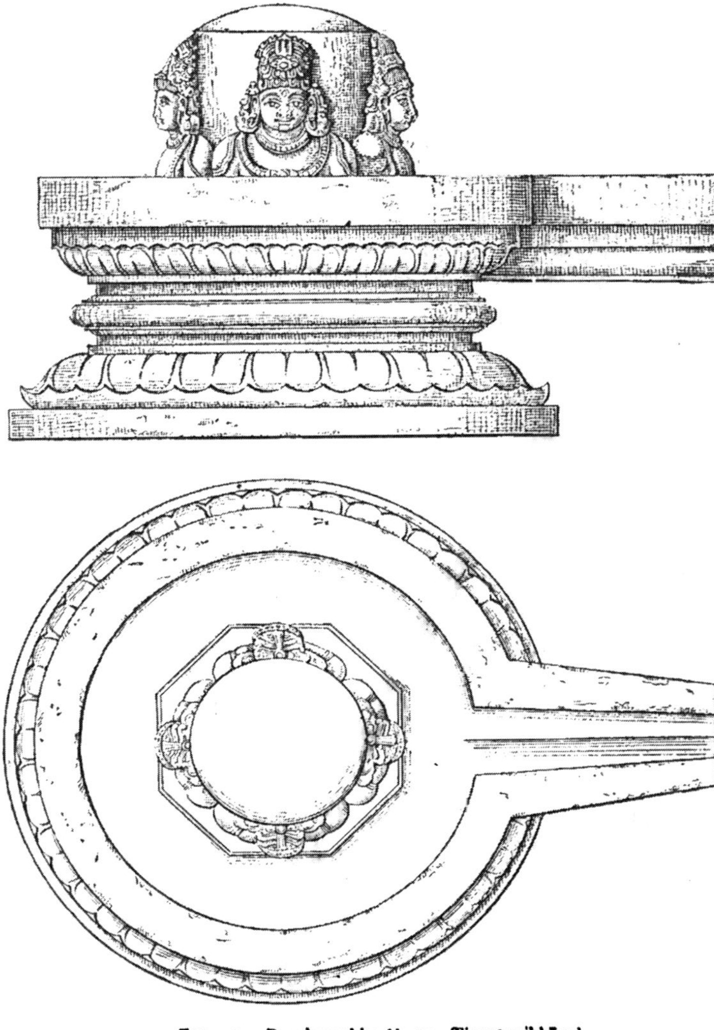

FIG. 47.- Panchamukha-*linga* ; Tiruvānaikkāval.

across the breast to the right side, its fingers gracefully pointing below, towards the left leg which is raised in a dancing posture. The position of this hand is known as *gaja-hasta*, "the elephant-trunk." The ecstatic and violent nature of the dance, described as Ānanda-tāndava in the sequel, whirling quickly round on one leg, placed on the back of the demon Musalagan or Apasmāra[1], is indicated by the matted hair *(jatā)* stretching out on both sides of the head in wavy lines one above the other and by the cloth, partly tied round the waist and partly thrown over the left shoulder, also flying in the air (fig. 48). The right hand which shows the *abhaya* has on its wrist a serpent, which is the usual ornament of Siva and may have 1, 3, 5 or 7 hoods. Another serpent, in the hand of the demon below, is explained by Mr. Havell (*Ideals of Indian Art*, p. 79) to be the corresponding wrist ornament on the left arm which had dropped down in the dance. We are told in the *Kāsyapa-Silpa* of the *Amsumat-Tantra* that a serpent with raised hood is to be shown playing near Apasmāra on his left side, the right hand of the demon pointing towards it *(vyāla-mudrā ?)*. The head of Siva wears peacock's feathers, or an ornament fashioned like them, which is a special characteristic of the image. The aureola *(prabhā)*, which every metallic image necessarily has, is, in this case, somewhat peculiar and significant, being surmounted all round with flames of fire similar to the one which is held in the pot or cup in one of the two left arms of the image.[2] The pedestal on which the figure rests is a double lotus flower placed back to back. Sometimes the *jatās* are not spread out but are tied and made up in the form of *jatāmakuta* (fig. 49).

Siva is said to dance in the evening in the presence of the goddess Pārvatī in order to relieve the sufferings of the *dēvas*. The dance of Natarāja is believed to symbolize the action of cosmic energy in creating, preserving and destroying the visible universe. The *Purānas* say that during these dances the whole congregation of gods, demigods and saints present themselves to render their obeisance to Siva. Hence the name Sabhāpati, "the lord of the

---

[1] Rai Bahadur V. Venkayya describes him s a hideous malignant dwarf, who sprang from the sacrificial fire of the *rishis* of the Dārukāvana forest and was subdued by Siva by being pressed under the tip of his foot (*S.I.I.* Vol. II, Introduction, p. 33, footnote). Perhaps he is the personification of the disease epilepsy wherein the victim is enveloped in complete mental darkness.

[2] The *Silparatna* remarks that the aureola of Natarāja represents the *ravi-mandala* or ' the sun's disc." This perhaps accounts for the flaming rays proceeding from the aureola.

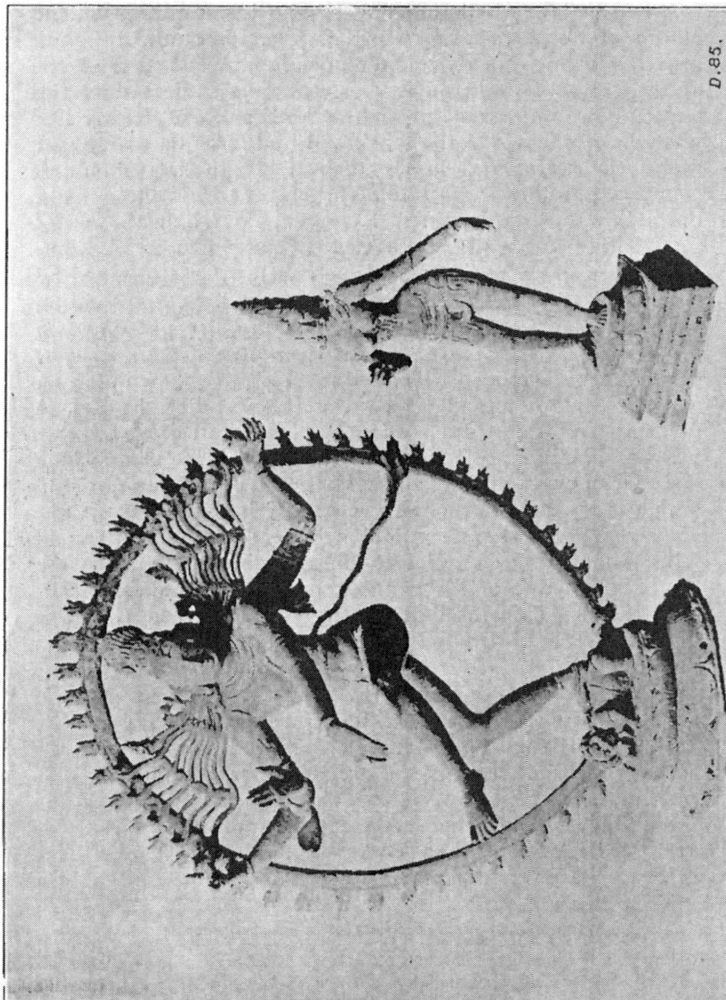

FIG. 48.—Nataraja (metal); Panchanadakkulam.

FIG. 49.—Naṭarāja (metal) ; Rāmēsvaram.

assembly" of gods.[1] The asterism Ārdrā occurring in the bright half of the solar month Mārgali (December-January) is sacred to Natarāja. All Siva temples celebrate a festival on that occasion by taking out in procession miniature representations of Natarāja or, where such do not exist, the chief processional image of Siva. In Chidambaram, of course, where the worship of Natarāja is the most prominent and where the *Sabhā-mandapa* (assembly hall) is covered with gold plate, the festival is the grandest held in the year.

Two main forms of dancing Siva may be distinguished: one with the raised leg as shown in the illustrations given above and the other with the same lifted up higher, to the level of the head. The latter is called Ūrdhva-tāndava—a dance which is locally believed to have been first performed by Siva at Tiruvālangādu near Arkōnam. The origin of this form of dance is as follows. There was once a dispute between Siva and his consort Kālī as to who was better in the art of dancing. Siva danced many a dance and Kālī successfully followed him; till at last, in order to suppress her pride, Siva lifted up one of his legs to the level of his crown and danced on. Kālī was too modest to imitate Siva in this performance and she accepted the superiority of Siva (fig. 50). Images of Natarāja are sometimes also seen with a small antelope prancing on his left side near the foot, the Gangā (Ganges) and the crescent decorating the head,[2] the sages Patanjali

[1] The *Kāranāgama* has the following about Sabhāpati:—

"On the top of the Kailāsa mountain, in front of the goddess Gaurī (Pārvatī) who is seated on a jewelled throne, Siva with the crescent on his head dances in the evenings. All the *dēvas* attend the dance; Brahmā plays on cymbals; Hari (Vishnu), on a *pataha*; Bhāratī (Sarasvatī), on the lute; the Sun and Moon, on flutes; Tumburu and Nārada supply vocal music; and Nandi and Kumāra (Skanda) beat drums." The *Mayamata* also mentions other gods and goddesses in the congregation, such as Vighnēsa (Vināyaka), Kālī and the Seven Mothers. It adds that Siva then performs the dance called *Bhujangatrāsita* with the serpent Karkōtaka on him; see Burgess's *Elura Cave Temples*, Plate XLIII, fig. 5.

[2] The description of the image of Ādavallān (i.e., "the expert dancer," Natarāja) given in the Tanjore Inscriptions, mentions "four arms, nine braids of hair *(jatā)*, the goddess Gangā-bhattārakī on the braided hair and seven flower garlands. The goddess Umāparamēsvarī who formed a part of the group was standing on a separate pedestal." Another image of a similar description in the same temple was Tanjai-Alagar with whom was connected also the figure of a Ganapati. Of the sages Patanjali and Vyāghrapāda who usually accompany the dancing image of Natarāja, the Tanjore Inscriptions describe the former as a solid image which measured "three-quarters and one-eighth (of a *mulam*) in height from the tail to the hoods *(phana)*. It had five hoods; one face in the midst of these hoods, one crown *(makuta)*, two divine arms, above the navel, a human body, and below the navel three coils"; (*S.I.I.*, Vol. II, Introduction,

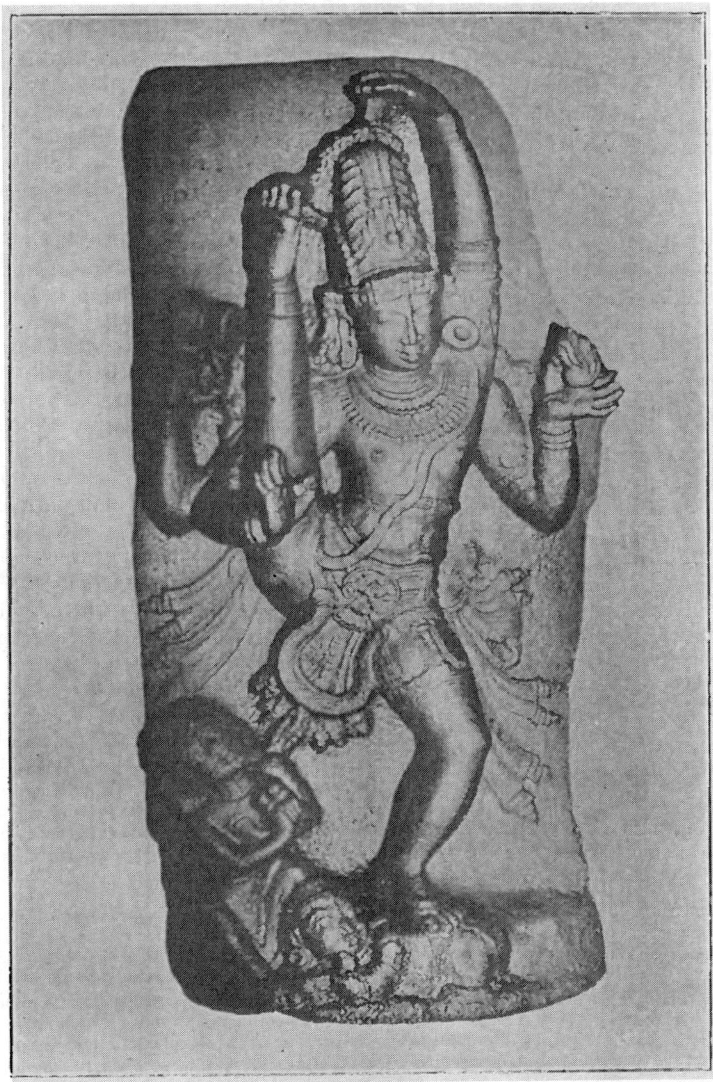

FIG. 50.—Ūrdhva-tāndava ; Tiruppanandāl.

(with the serpent-body, fig. 51) and Vyāghrapāda (with tiger's feet, fig. 52) worshipping on either side and the goddess Pārvatī standing on the left.

The *Āgamas* speak of seven dancing postures of Siva.

ĀNANDA-TĀNDAVA. The first, called Ānanda-tāndava or the joyous dance, has been described above.

SANDHYĀ-TĀNDAVA. The second is his evening dance Sandhyā-tāndava.[1] In this form the demon Apasmāra is absent and the symbols in the two left arms are the peacock-feathers and the pose of wonder called *vismaya*.

UMĀ-TĀNDAVA. The third is the Umā-tāndava, i.e., dance with his consort Umā. In this Siva has two more arms, the additional right hand holding the trident *(trisūla)* and the three left hands exhibiting the skull, *vismaya*, and the *gaja-hasta*. The left leg is placed on Apasmāra and the right leg is stretched towards the left, and the goddess Umā stands on the left side.

GAURĪ-TĀNDAVA. The fourth, Gaurī-tāndava, is almost similar to the first, but in one of the left hands of the god is held a serpent. Nandi stands on the right side and Gaurī (Pārvatī) is on the left.[2]

KĀLIKĀ-TĀNDAVA. In the fifth form, called Kālikā-tāndava, the god has only two eyes, but eight arms. Three of the right arms hold the trident, noose and kettle-drum and the corresponding left hold the skull, fire-pot and the bell; the two remaining arms exhibit the *abhaya* on the right and *gaja-hasta* on the left (fig. 53).[3]

TRIPURA-TĀNDAVA. The dance of Siva, with sixteen arms and as many symbols, having Gaurī and Skanda on the left and right sides respectively,[4] receives the name Tripura-tāndava.

SAMHĀRA-TĀNDAVA. The last dance called Samhāra-tāndava "the death-dance" shows the god with three eyes and eight arms. The left leg is placed on Apasmāra and the right leg is raised. In the right

---

p. 33). This description closely agrees with the figure of Patanjali on the eastern *gōpura* of the Natarāja temple at Chidambaram. On the same *gōpura* is the image of Vyāghrapāda in which the sage is represented as having tiger's claws on both his hands and feet. The sage is carrying on his right shoulder a hook and a flower basket.

---

[1] According to the *Silpasangraha* and the *Mayamata*, the dance is performed under the *vata* or the banyan tree.

[2] This same dance is described in the *Mayamata* as *Bhujangalalita* in which by quick changes in the position of the legs, the fire in the hand is blown into a blaze, and the braided locks are spread out into five, seven or nine. On the left side stands Vishnu in place of Gaurī, and on the right Nandi.

[3] In the illustrations the weapons and symbols are seen just as they are mentioned in the *Āgamas*. The position of the legs in the one, and the *abhaya* and the *gaja-hasta* poses in the other, are, however, reversed.

[4] The *Silparatnā* says that Skanda stands on the same side as Gaurī holding her by the hand, and shows fear, love and wonder in his face.

FIG. 51. – Patanjali; Chidambaram.

FIG. 52.—Vyāghrapāda; Chidambaram.

FIG. 53. -Kālikā-tāndava (metal); Nallūr.

hands are seen the *abhaya*, trident, noose and the kettle-drum; the left hands exhibit the skull and the fire-pot and the postures *vismaya* and *gaja-hasta*. On the right and left sides respectively are Nandi and Gaurī.

Other *Āgamas* again, refer to 108 dancing forms of Siva nine of which are said to be celebrated. Of these latter the only one that deserves to be noted is that in which the god has his right leg raised straight up so as to reach the top of the crown *(ushnisha)*. Perhaps, this is the Ūrdhva-tāndava, described already. He may have four, eight or sixteen arms.

ŪRDHVA-TANDAVA.

Chidambaram; its history.

No account of Natarāja could be complete without a short history of Chidambaram and its temple. Tradition has it that years ago a king from the north, called Simhavarman, came south on a pilgrimage. All this part of the country was then one huge forest. The king happened to bathe in a well, and immediately found himself transformed into a bright golden figure. He assumed the name Hiranyavarman "the gold-armoured" on that account and covered with gold the Siva temple which he discovered near that well. It is stated that before him the sages Patanjali and Vyāghrapāda had worshipped there. Simhavarman and Hiranyavarman are Pallava names and denote that the origin of the temple may be roughly traced to that period. Historically, it was the Chōla king Parāntaka I, surnamed Vīra-Chōla and Vīra-Nārāyana (A.D. 907 to about 951) who covered the Chidambaram temple with gold, perhaps for the first time. Successive Chōla kings, after him, are known to have added to the grandeur of it[1]. A later Pallava chief of the thirteenth century A.D. called Perunjingadēva boasts of having conquered the four quarters and utilized the booty secured, in decorating the eastern *gōpura* of the Chidambaram temple which he had himself constructed.[2] The great Vijayanagara king Krishnadēvarāya of the sixteenth century A.D. built the north *gōpura* of the same temple after his victorious return from

---

[1] The devotion of Rājarāja I to the god at Chidambaram and the rich presents which he must have made to the temple there, evidently earned for him the titles Srī-Rājarāja and Sivapādasēkhara; Rai Bahadur Venkayya thinks that Rājarāja built at Tanjore the big temple of Rājarājēsvara (i.e., Brihadīsvara) in order to commemorate the conferring of these titles. He consecrated therein the god Siva and called him Ādavallān, i.e., the expert dancer, after the famous Natarāja of Chidambaram.

[2] It is from this *gōpura* that the best illustrations are secured. The *gōpura* is very rich in sculptures and has various forms of Siva and his attendant gods. In this *gōpura* are also found illustrations of the 108 postures in dancing, mentioned in the *Bhāratīya-Nātyasāstra* (vide Madras Epigraphical Report for 1913–14, Plates I to IV). They are appropriately meant to be connected with Natarāja the king of dancers.

a campaign in the north. It is well known that as a sacred place of pilgrimage Chidambaram is intimately connected with the Saiva saint Mānikyavāchaka (Mānikkavāsagar), the Pariah saint Nandanār—both of whom attained their salvation there—and with the Saiva philosopher and scholar Appaya-Dīkshita who was much devoted to that temple. The place is mentioned in the Saiva hymns of the *Dēvāram*, in which it is called Tillai. The 3,000 Brāhmana families of Tillai (which may have once lived there but have at present dwindled down to a few hundreds) claim Siva to be one of them and worship Natarāja as their family deity.

VI

. The *Āgamas* mention, as already stated,[1] twenty-five sportive forms *(līlā-mūrtis)* of Siva, most of which are usually met with in South-Indian temples. One of the more important of these is Dakshināmūrti. In Chōla temples this image generally occupies a niche in the south wall of the central shrine. Dakshināmūrti or Dharma-Vyākhyānamūrti is the form of Siva engaged in *yōga* or philosophic contemplation. Once upon a time Daksha, the father-in-law of Siva, insulted him and his consort Umā, by not inviting them to a sacrifice which he was performing. Umā nevertheless went uninvited to her father's house, but being grossly neglected jumped into the sacrificial fire-pit and destroyed herself. Siva was furious; he created out of a lock of his hair the terrible Vīrabhadra (see below, p. 155) who destroyed Daksha. Siva then retired to a forest with the resolve not to marry again and sat underneath a banyan tree deeply engaged in meditation. The gods were much concerned; for it meant that the world would loose the benefit of Siva's direct intervention in its affairs. They accordingly induced Kāma,[2] the god of love, to stir up once again in the mind of Siva the dormant embers of love. The fool-hardy Kāma incautiously approached the god engaged in meditation and shot his flowery arrows at him and hit him. Siva then opened his eye of fire and looked straight at Kāma, when lo! he was at once reduced to a heap of ashes.[3] Still Kāma had succeeded. For, soon afterwards Siva gave up his

DAKSHINĀMŪRTI.

[1] Above, p. 76, footnote 1.

[2] Described above, p. 62.

[3] This incident has given rise to the recognition of another sportive form of Siva called Kāmāri or Kāmadahanamūrti. The scene is depicted on one of the pillars of an unfinished *mandapa* near the tank in the Ēkāmrēsvara temple at Conjeeveram. According to the *Kāranāgama*, Kāmadahanamūrti has four arms in which are seen the *abhaya*, *varada*, a deer and the *tanka*. He is seated on a lotus pedestal and is fierce in appearance.

penance and married once again Umā, who had now incarnated as Pārvatī, the beautiful daughter of Himavat (the Himalayas). This is the story of Dakshināmūrti.[1] He is always conceived to be a youthful teacher, seated beneath a banyan tree, teaching aged pupils and removing their doubts by his very silence. The general posture of the images of Dakshināmūrti show him with his right leg bent vertically at the knee and placed on the body of the dark demon Apasmāra[2] and the left leg bent across so as to rest upon the right thigh. He has a calm countenance, indicative of perfect peace within. His matted locks are either dishevelled or are formed into a *jatāmakuta* tied together by a serpent (fig. 54). The body is besmeared with ashes and all the usual ornaments of Siva decorate him. The sages Nārada, Jamadagni, Vasishtha and Bhrigu sit at his feet on the right side, receiving instruction, while Bharadvāja, Saunaka, Agastya and Bhārgava sit on the left. The bull-vehicle of the god, the denizens of the forest, *Kinnaras* and other demi-gods are also seen on the Kailāsa mountain on which the god is seated.[3] His right fore-arm points the *jnāna-mudrā* (the pose conveying philosophical knowledge) and the back arm holds the rosary (or, the serpent); the left fore-arm shows the boon-conferring *(varada)* attitude or is sometimes freely stretched, the back of the palm resting in either case on the left knee. Some illustrations show a book in the place of the *varada* posture. The remaining hand on the left side holds the fire-pot, the deer, the kettle-drum or the rosary. When Dakshināmūrti holds in his fore-arms the lute *(vīnā)* and changes the posture of his left leg—apparently for keeping the *vīnā* in position—he is called Vīnādhara-Dakshināmūrti (fig. 55). Jnānamūrti is another form of the same god in which the symbol *jnāna-mudrā* of the right fore-arm is raised close to the heart with the palm of the hand turned inwards. The name Yōgamūrti (or Yōga-Dakshināmūrti) is applied when the legs crossing each other from the root of the thigh are held in position by the belt *yōgapatta*, passing round the waist and the

VĪNADHARA-DAKSHINĀMŪRTI, JNĀNAMŪRTI and YŌGAMŪRTI.

---

[1] Havell, *Ideals of Indian Art*, p. 83f.

[2] The *Silpasangraha* mentions a serpent playing by the side of Apasmāra.

[3] The description of Dakshināmūrti given in the Tanjore inscriptions is very interesting and instructive. They say that the mountain on which the god is seated "had two peaks on which there were two *Kinnaras* and two *Kinnaris*. Under the foot of the god was Musalagan. On the mountain were four *rishis*, a snake, two *Karnaprāvritas* (i.e., devotees of Siva (?) mentioned in the *Rāmāyana*, who had ear-lobes with holes big enough to allow their hands to be passed through in the act of worshipping) and a tiger. A banyan tree was also on the mountain and had nine main branches and forty-two minor ones. A wallet was suspended from the tree and a bunch of peacock's feathers was one of the accompaniments of the god"; *S.I.I.*, Vol. II, Introduction, p. 33.

FIG. 54.—Dakshināmūrti ; Āvūr.

FIG. 55.—Vīṇādhara-Dakshiṇāmūrti ; Chidambaram.

fore-legs, a little below the knee. The front arms are in this case, stretched out and rest freely on the knees, while the back arms hold the rosary and the water pot. The illustration (fig. 56) differs, however, in the symbols. In this, the upper hands hold the water-pot and the antelope and the lower hands the rosary (with *jnāna-mudrā*) and the book. A fine old picture (fig. 57) coming from Tiruvengavāsal (Pudukkōttai State) shows Dakshināmūrti in a different position and with different symbols.

VII

Lingōdbhava "the *linga*-manifestation," is a familiar figure of Siva seen on the west wall of the central shrine of Siva temples built in Chōla times. As his name implies, he is represented within a huge *linga*, the portion of the feet below the ankles being hidden in the *linga*. Brahmā in the form of a swan is seen soaring up on the left side of Siva ; while, on the right side, Vishnu is delving below into the depths of the earth in the form of a boar.[1] Also these gods (i.e., Brahmā and Vishnu) in their true glory stand on either side of Siva with folded hands. The figure emanating from the middle of the *linga* (fig. 58) has four hands like Chandrasēkhara (described below) and holds in its back arms the axe and the antelope and in the front hands, the *abhaya* and the *varada* postures. In the illustration given, the left hand is, however, seen resting freely on the waist. In the Tanjore inscriptions, Lingōdbhava is mentioned by the name Lingapurānadēva, i.e., the god of the Linga-*Purāna* which describes the greatness of the *linga*. The story runs that a dispute arose between Brahmā and Vishnu as to who is the greater of the two. Siva told them that whoever first saw the top or the bottom of his own fiery *linga*-form[2] and came back to report, he would be considered the greater. Brahmā soared on his swan to see the top of the Siva-*linga*, while Vishnu as a boar dug down and down to see its bottom. Ages passed away and neither came to his goal. At last Brahmā saw one *kētaki* flower coming down. It had fallen from Siva's head ages ago. Brahmā suborned it to give false evidence and then came back and uttered a lie, saying that he had seen the top of the *linga*, citing the *kētaki* flower as his witness. Siva knew the lie and cursed Brahmā that he should thenceforward go without any worship in temples. Brahmā had five heads at this time.

LINGŌD-BHAVA.

[1] The swan and the boar are in some pictures found to be half-man and half-animal.

[2] On the east main *gōpura* of the Chidambaram temple is an image of Lingōdbhava surrounded by flames of fire.

FIG. 56.—Yōga-Dakshināmūrti ; Conjeeveram.

FIG. 57.—Dakshināmūrti ; Tiruvengavāsal.

FIG. 58.—Lingōdbhava ; Tanjore.

Siva also cut off the head which uttered the lie.[1] The flower *ketaki* too, which abetted the crime, was excluded from the flowers dear to Siva. On an apology being offered; the latter was however accepted, as a special case, during the worship on the night of the Sivarātri festival which falls on the fourteenth day of the dark half of Māgha (January-February) in each year and is held sacred in honour of the *linga*-manifestation of Siva.

Perhaps, images called Ēkapādamūrti or Ēkapāda-Trimūrti, in which the gods Brahmā and Vishnu, with folded hands and characteristic symbols, are represented as proceeding out of the body of Siva at his waist as in the Tiruvottiyūr image (fig. 59) or from behind his knee as in the image from Tiruvānaikkāval (fig. 60) are either developments of Lingōdbhava wherein the superiority of Siva over the two other members of the Hindu Triad was established, or an invention of the Indian sculptor in which is symbolized the underlying unity of the three gods.[2] The *Kāranāgama* mentions Ēkapāda mūrti as one of the sportive forms of Siva and describes him as having one foot, three eyes and four arms in which are seen the *tanka* and deer and the *varada* and the *abhaya* postures. On the right and left sides of Siva, almost touching his shoulders, are Brahmā and Vishnu holding their symbolical weapons in two hands and worshipping Siva with the other two. ĒKAPĀDA MŪRTI.

The single foot which is the characteristic feature of these figures, is, in the case of the Tiruvānaikkāval image, placed on the back of the bull. In it are also seen the vehicle of Brahmā, viz., the swan, at the right bottom and, at the corresponding left bottom, the standing Garuda vehicle of Vishnu and a sage—perhaps Nārada. Apparently Ēkapādamūrti has to be connected with Ajaikapād, a name given in the Rig-Vēda to one of the Ēkādasa-Rudras.[3]

VIII

The story of Lingōdbhava introduces us to another form of Siva, known as Bhikshātana, very often seen in South-Indian temples. When Siva cut off one of the heads of BHIKSHATANA.

---

[1] The *Kāranāgama* mentions a sportive form of Siva cutting off one of the heads of Brahmā. The image is stated to have four arms holding the thunder-bolt and the axe in the right hand and the trident and Brahmā's skull in the left.

[2] Accordingly, we sometimes find Vishnu occupying the central place. On p. 73 above, footnote 1, it was noted that the goddess Gāyatrī was absorbed into the centre of the *linga* while Brahmā and Vishnu entered the sides of it.

[3] See Nagendra Natha Vasu's *Mayūrabhanja*, Introduction, p. xxxi.

FIG. 59.—Ēkapāda-Trimūrti ; Tiruvottiyūr.

FIG. 60.—Ēkapāda-Trimūrti ; Tiruvānaikkāval.

Brahmā, he incurred the sin of killing a Brāhmana; and the skull of Brahmā, it is stated, stuck to Siva's palm and would not drop down. In order to get rid of the sin and this incriminating skull, Siva had to wander about as a naked beggar *(bhikshātana)* until he reached the place still known as Brahma-kapālam, on the slopes of the Himalayas, where he was released from the sin and the skull fell down of its own accord.[1] Local chronicles connect Bhikshātana with the Valuvūr and Tirutturaippūndi temples in the Tanjore district, and mention that the god Siva assumed a beautiful naked form and came out as a wandering beggar to test the fidelity of the wives of certain sages of the Dārukāvana forest, who were proud of their chastity. At the same time Vishnu is stated to have taken up the form of Mōhinī in order to tempt the sages. In accordance with this story, we occasionally see naked figures of women and of Mōhinī (fig. 61) depicted in close proximity to Bhikshātana. The tip of the lower right hand of the image touches the mouth of an antelope. The upper right hand holds the kettle-drum. A trident with peacock-feathers (not seen in the illustration fig. 62)[2]—or a big bunch of them placed across the shoulder, decorates the upper left arm, while the lower left, shows the boon-conferring posture. In it is also seen the *kapāla* (skull). A serpent encircles his waist and he stands on sandals. The right leg is slightly bent *(kunchita)* and the left is firmly placed in the attitude of one inclined to walk on. Above the right ankle is tied a bell *(bhringipāda)* which gives notice of the approach of the divine mendicant. A demon called Kundōdara, with protruding teeth, stands on the left side of the god, carrying on his head a begging bowl. The Bhikshātana-mūrti at Pērūr has eight arms and holds different weapons in each of them[3]. A fine figure of Bhikshātana (in Tamil, Pichchāndār) is found in a niche on the south wall of the central shrine of the big temple at Tanjore. A copper image of this god, with a goblin carrying the begging bowl and an antelope following, is said to have been presented to that temple by Lōkamahādēvī, the chief queen of Rājarāja I. This god was to witness every day the *Sribali* ceremony conducted in the temple.

[1] The *Mahābhārata* refers to a similar story and states that a *rishi* called Mahōdara got himself relieved of the skull of a giant that had stuck to his knee, by bathing in the sacred tank called Kapālamōchana-tīrtha.

[2] This image is published in the Archæological Survey Report, Madras, for 1911–12, Plate I, fig. 2, but without the two accompanying figures of the deer and the demon.

[3] The *Mayamata* says that this form of Siva may have four, six or eight arms.

FIG. 61.—Mōhinī (metal); Valuvūr.

FIG. 62.—Bhikshâtanamûrti (metal); Valuvûr.

IX

Kankālamūrti is a form closely allied to Bhikshātana and almost similar in appearance. According to the *Mayamata*, Kankālamūrti is draped in a fine cloth and is surrounded by lovely women. In his upper right hand he holds the peacock's feathers and skeleton *(kankāla)* and in the upper left the *tanka*. A serpent is coiled round his loins; and he has a knife stuck into the girdle on the right side of his waist (figs. 63 and 64). He is generally attended by demons. Birds and beasts follow him in expectation of getting something to eat from his hands. The description given of Kankālamūrti in the *Kāsyapa-Silpa* of the *Amsumat-Tantra* is different. He has a *jatāmakuta*[1] decorated with serpents, the crescent-moon and flowers; he is holding the kettle-drum in his left fore-arm and a stick (to beat it with) in the corresponding right; the other right hand is in the pose *simha-karna* and touches the mouth of the antelope, while the left carries a bunch of peacock's feathers on a staff. He also wears a necklace of skeletons *(kankāla)* which according to the Āditya-*Purāna* are supposed to be those of Vishnu in his various incarnations. Sometimes he may be represented also as carrying on his shoulder a *kankāla* (skeleton) tied by a rope to the staff. KANKĀLA-MŪRTI

X

The form of Siva, decorated as a bridegroom, is called Kalyānasundaramūrti or Vāivāhikamūrti. Siva in this form is represented as a fair youth, with three eyes and four arms. He is clothed in the best of garments and wears a garland of blue lilies. On his right side stands Pārvatī, his bride, whose right hand he holds with his own. In his back hands are seen the symbols, *tanka* (or sometimes the axe) and the black buck. The left lower hand shows the boon-giving posture. His matted locks are made up in the fashion of a *jatāmakuta* on which is stuck the crescent of the moon. The general posture of the god is what is called *samabhanga*, or the medium bend, wherein the figure stands with the right leg slightly bent and the left leg placed firmly on the ground. The goddess on the right side is represented as a fully developed maiden. She has only two hands, one of which holds a lily. Brahmā, having in his four hands the rosary, water-pot, KALYĀNA-SUNDARA-MŪRTI.

---

[1] The braided hair *(jatā)* of Bhikshātana, on the other hand, is generally found in illustrations, arranged in a circle. *Jatāmakuta* is the arrangement of the *jatas* in the form of a *makuta* or crown. The former is, perhaps, what is known in the Silpa-works as *jatāmandala*.

FIG. 63.—Kankálamûrti (metal); Tenkâsi.

FIG. 64.—Kankālamūrti ; Dhārāsuram.

FIG. 65.—Kalyānasundara ; Madura.

the sacrificial ladle *(srik)* and the spoon *(sruva)* (or, the book), is seated on a lotus flower in front of a square fire-pit facing northwards, and offering oblations to the sacrificial fire, which is burning in front with five flames. Mēnakā and Himavat, the parents of the goddess, are standing to her right, carrying a golden pot, from which they pour water into the hands of Siva and Pārvatī in token of giving away their daughter in marriage to him. The sages Sanaka and Sanandana stand to the left of the god with folded hands. Vishnu is present with the whole congregation of gods and goddesses. This description of Kalyānasundara is found in all its details in a figure from Elephanta. The *Kāsyapa-Silpa* of the *Amsumat-Tantra* and the *Silpasangraha* say that Vishnu in the *tribhanga* attitude faces south and stands on the north side of the sacrificial fire-pit with conch and discus in his back arms. He pours with his two other hands water from a gold pot into the hands of Siva and Pārvatī (fig. 65). The *Mayamata* describes Pārvatī as standing by the side of Lakshmī. It looks as if Mēnakā and Himavat are sometimes substituted by Lakshmī and Vishnu. A fine image of Kalyānasundara comes from the Chidambaram temple (fig. 66). Svayamvarā is the name given in the *Silparatna* to the figure of Pārvatī as a bride. She holds a garland of flowers and walks towards Sambhu (Siva) to choose him as her husband.

XI

Sōmāskanda is the most common of all the sportive forms of Siva. Its design is as old as the Pallava period and it may be found on the back wall of the *sanctum* immediately behind the *linga* in almost every temple which pretends to belong to that age. The group, e.g., is found engraved on the back wall of a niche in the second storey of the Dharmarāja-*ratha* at Mahābalipuram which, according to an inscription cut on the lintel, was apparently intended to be a shrine for the Siva-*linga* called Atyantakāma-Pallavēsvara. It is also seen on the back wall of the Siva shrine facing the sea, in the "Shore Temple." The Sāluvankuppam cave, called Atiranachanda-Pallavēsvara, also has the same image. A similar panel is also found in the Kailāsanātha temple at Kānchī. Later Chōla temples, however, do not show any such panel on the wall behind the *linga*. On one and the same pedestal are seen Siva and Umā with the child Skanda standing (or seated) between them. Both the god and the goddess are seated comfortably *(sukhāsana)*, with one leg (right in the case of Siva and left in the case of Pārvatī) hanging down

SŌMĀSKANDA.

FIG. 66.—Kalyānasundara and Svayamvarā; Chidambaram.

FIG. 67.—Sōmāskanda (metal); Sivankūdal.

and the other bent crosswise so as to lie flat on the pedestal. The god holds in his upper hands the *tanka* (or, the axe) and the deer and in the lower exhibits the *varada* and the *abhaya* postures. The goddess holds a lily in her right hand and shows the *varada* or the *kataka* pose[1] in her left (fig. 67). She may sometimes also be represented as resting the palm of her left hand on the pedestal by the side of her left thigh while the right hand, as before, holds the lily. Skanda has the crown *karandamakuta* and holds in one of his hands a flower, a wood-apple or a mango. According to the *Kāranāgama* the group must be flanked by two standing or seated figures called Bhōga-Sakti and Vīra-Sakti on the left and right sides respectively.[2] It is also stated that the right side of the pedestal on which the god sits is to be slightly higher than the left.

A photograph from Mahābalipuram (fig. 68) is worth noting in this connexion. It shows Siva in the comfortably seated posture. In his upper hands, however, the symbols, evidently of *tanka* and the deer, are missing. The right lower is in the posture of *abhaya* and the left lower in that of *kataka*. It is also possible that the latter is resting freely on the thigh. Pārvatī is seated on Siva's left side, turning her face towards him and holding the child Skanda on her knee. In the upper corners are seen flying dwarfs, apparently holding flywhisks in their hands. The whole group is flanked by two four-armed gods raising respectively the upper left and right arms and pointing them towards Siva.

Among the Mahābalipuram sculptures we find still another scene of Saiva pictures apparently allied to Sōmāskanda just

SUKHĀSANA OR UMĀ-SAHITA.

described, viz., Sukhāsana or Umāsahita mentioned in footnote 1 on p. 76. Here, on a pedestal supported by two lion-pillars and the recumbant bull between them, is a seated figure of Siva with a robe of ornamental fringes, hanging loosely from above his right shoulder. In his right upper hand he holds a furious serpent. What the position of his left upper hand indicates, is not clear. Of the two other hands, the left lower rests freely on his right leg and the left thigh, while the right lower exhibits a position of the fingers which suggests that the god must have held some weapon. The high *jatāmakuta*, the divine halo (circle of light) round the face, the necklaces, pendants, ear-rings, waist-band, rings on hands and a thick

[1] The actual position of the hand as described in the *Āgamas*, however, is *simha-karna* or "lion's ear" with the fingers slightly closing on the palmside.

[2] Siva is supposed to have three *Saktis* attached to him, viz., Yōga-Sakti, Bhōga-Sakti and Vīra-Sakti; see below, p. 185, footnote 1.

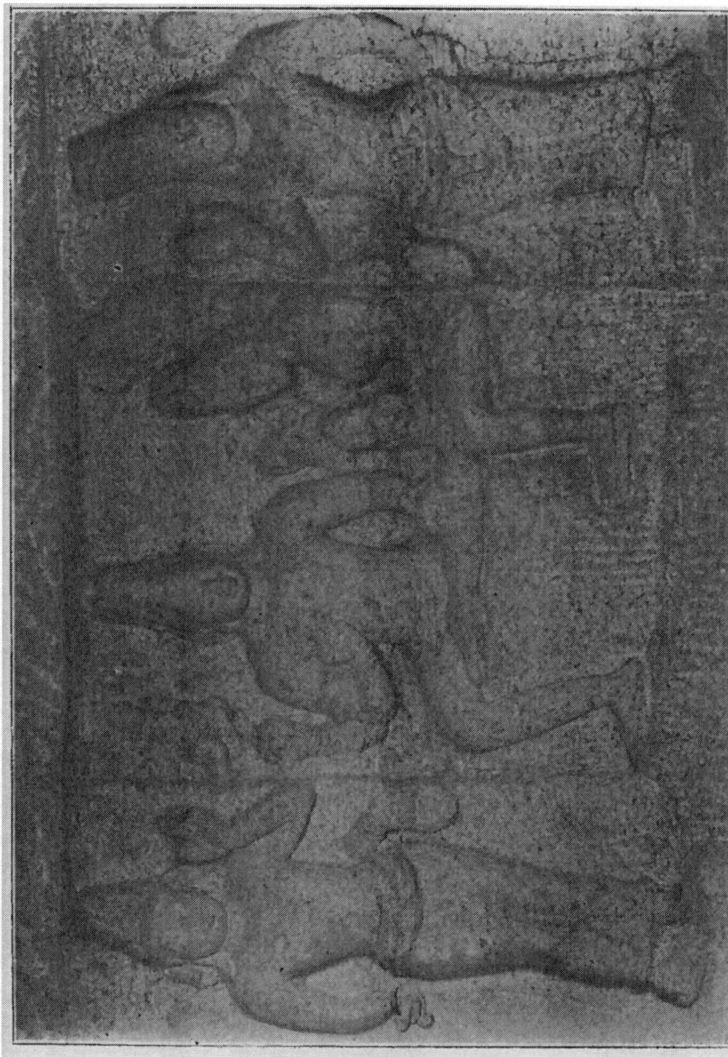

FIG. 68.—Sōmāskanda ; Seven Pagodas.

FIG. 69.—Umâsahita; Seven Pagodas.

chord across the breast representing the Brahmanical thread *yajnōpavita*, are the other jewels seen on the figure of Siva. To the right of Siva's shoulder is Brahmā with the water-pot in one hand and the erect rosary in the other. The sacred thread of Brahmā has four strings. Between the heads of Brahmā and Siva is a circular disc which perhaps represents the Sun. Near the left shoulder of Siva is Vishnu holding the discus and the conch in his two upper hands. Here again, the position of the two lower hands is not clear. The sacred thread of Vishnu has three strings. His crown though high like that of the two other gods is shaped somewhat differently. Pārvatī (Siva's consort) with the child Skanda on her right lap is seated on the left side of Siva. Her left foot is placed on the back of the couchant bull. She as well as her child have only two arms each. Close to her left foot, behind the bull, is a female attendant of Pārvatī, who raises her right hand resting it on the back of the bull. Between the head of the goddess and that of Vishnu is seen what is perhaps to be interpreted as the crescent of the Moon, corresponding to the Sun on the other side. But the short handle attached to it at the bottom seems to show that it may be an umbrella of honour held over the head of the goddess (fig. 69). A similar group, called Umā-Mahēsvara according to Hēmādri, consists of Siva and Pārvatī, the former having eight faces and two hands. The left hand of the god is stretched over the shoulder of the goddess and the right hand of the goddess over that of the god. The *Kāranāgama* describing this group states that the goddess Pārvatī should be seated on the left side of Siva with the bull in front of them, Indra and other gods behind, Vishnu and Brahmā on the sides and the devotees Bhringi, Nārada, Bāna, Bhairava, Ganapati, Skanda and Vīrēsvara in the eight cardinal points. Rai Bahadur Venkayya considered this description to be that of Rishabhavāhana (Vrishavāhana)[1] mentioned in the next paragraph.

UMĀ-MAHĒSVARA.

XII

VRISHĀRŪDHA.

Vrishārūdha is a figure of Siva seated on the bull with the right leg hanging down and the left bent so as to rest on the bull. He has Ganapati on his right side and Gaurī on his left.[2] He holds in his two upper hands the *tanka* and the antelope. When, however, Siva is made to stand leaning

---

[1] *S.I.I.*, Vol. II, Introduction, p. 33, footnote 1.

[2] The *Silparatna* and the *Kāsyapa-Silpa* state that more often Gaurī is seen on the right side of the god.

VRISHAVĀHANA. against the bull and is not mounted on it, the *Kāsyapa-Silpa* calls him Vrishavāhana. In this case the elbow *(kūrpara)* of the right hand of Siva rests on the head of the bull as in the illustrations (figs. 70 and 71).[1] The *Mayamata* also gives the same description, but adds that the bull stands behind the seat on which the god and goddess sit. The right lower hand of Siva holds the trident while the two upper hands hold the axe and the deer.

XIII

CHANDRASĒKHARAMŪRTI. Chandrasēkharamūrti[2] (the crescent-crested lord) may, according to the *Kāsyapa-Silpa* of the *Amsumat-Tantra*, be represented in two different forms, either alone or in company of the goddess Gaurī. When alone, he stands on the pedestal with level feet *(samapāda)*, holding the antelope and the kettle-drum (or, axe) in his back arms and presenting the *abhaya* and the *varada* postures in the fore-arms. The crescent decorates the *jatāmakuta* of the god, either on its right side or on the left. In other respects the image is a pleasing representation (fig. 72) of the general form of Rudra described above. When accompanied by the goddess he may also be seated (fig. 73). The right lower hand shows the *abhaya* posture and the left lower passes round the back of the yielding goddess and touches her breasts. Some *Āgamas* do not permit the hand to be stretched so far, but only up to the left arm of the goddess. The illustration from Bāgali (fig. 74) answers to this description but holds the trident and the kettle-drum in the upper hands instead of the axe and the deer. The goddess also with her right hand touches the right side of the waist-band of the god from the back and holds a flower in her left. She may also be seen passing her hand over his shoulder. Such figures of Chandrasēkhara are called Ālinganamūrti or the embracing form. They are also known as Pradōshamūrti, since in all well-maintained Siva temples,

---

1 The illustrations given show two and four hands respectively for Siva, who standing with his legs crossed and leaning against the back of the bull, has the *kūrpara* of his right hand placed on the head of the bull. A fine image from Ceylon figured as No. 29 in Part II of *Visvakarma* is evidently one of Vrishārūdha as described in the *Mayamata*. The trident in the right lower hand, the bull and the goddess are missing.

2 The great Chōla king Rājarāja I is represented in the Tanjore inscriptions to have been devoted particularly to this form of Siva. The figures of the king and of Chandrasēkhara receiving worship from him, were set up by the manager of the temple before the close of the 29th year of that king, i.e., before A.D. 1013-14.

Fig. 70.—Vrishavâhana; Chidambaram.

FIG. 71.—Vrishavāhana (metal); Vēdāranyam.

FIG. 72.—Chandrasekhara (metal); Tiruvottiyūr.

FIG. 73.—Chandrasêkhara; Tanjore.

FIG. 74.—Chandrasékhara (Âlinganamûrti) ; Bâgali

the image is carried about in procession in the evenings *(pradōsha)*.

XIV

ARDHANĀRI. The hermaphrodite or the Ardhanāri form of Siva is perhaps to be traced to the conception of the Sākta doctrine that only when combined with Sakti is Siva capable of discharging his divine functions.[1] The idea of representing a male ornament in the right lobe of Siva and a female ornament in his left lobe must, already, have been due to the belief in the inseparable union of the masculine and feminine elements in the Creator. The artistic conception of a purely philosophical idea has thus resulted in an image of which the left half represents the woman (Pārvatī) and the right half, the male (Siva). The jewellery on the image is similarly distinguished in every detail; those on the left side being purely feminine ornaments and those on the right, ornaments appropriate to males. The drapery on the right side is the tiger's skin of Siva reaching only to the knee, while on the left side it is the finely embroidered muslin *(dukūla)* suitable for the goddess Pārvatī, and stretching down to her ankle. Of the four hands, the two right show a hatchet and the posture of protection; the two left are richly decorated with wristlets, the upper one holding a flower and the lower one being stretched down to the waist (fig. 75). The *Kāsyapa-Silpa*, however, says that the right lower hand may be placed on the head of the bull. Some images show only three hands, two on the right and one on the left. In that case the right upper hand holds the axe while the lower right rests on the head of the bull. The figure stands leaning gracefully against the back of the bull, bending its body above the waist. Of the two other illustrations given, one is from the Nāgēsvara temple at Kumbakōnam (fig. 76) and the other is from a niche on the north wall of the Tanjore temple (fig. 77). Sometimes images of Ardhanāri may have only two arms. Thus in the temple at Tiruchchengōdu (Salem district), dedicated to Ardhanāri, the image (fig. 78) has only two hands, the right one holding a staff with the lower end resting on the waist, and the left placed on the left hip. It may be noted that the hair on the head of this image is done up in the fashion peculiar to images of Krishna. An illustration coming from Dhārāsuram shows eight arms, three visible faces (with perhaps two others

[1] The popular story connected with the origin of this form is given below (p. 165), under Bhringīsa.

FIG. 75.—Ardhanāri; Madura.

FIG. 76.—Ardhanāri ; Kumbakōnam.

FIG. 77.—Ardhanāri; Tanjore.

FIG. 78.—Ardhanāri; Tiruchchengōdu.

behind) and a circle of light in the back ground. This is apparently an unusual form (fig. 79). Still another unusual form comes from Tiruvādi near Tanjore, in which the right half is woman and the left half male (fig. 80).

XV

A similar composite image of Siva is the one called Harihara or Sankaranārāyana. In this image the left half is Vishnu and the right half Siva. Accordingly we see on the left side of the figures of Harihara, the conch, the pearl-necklace, the mark *Srivatsa* and the brilliant ear-ring characteristic of Vishnu and on the right side the skull, the garland of bones, the river Gangā, the serpent coil of the ear-ring and the trident or axe, characteristic of Siva. So too the colour of the body is blue on the left and white on the right. Similarly, Garuda, the vehicle of Vishnu, may be seen standing on the left and the bull of Siva on the right. Sankaranāyinārkōyil in the Tinnevelly district has a famous temple dedicated to this combined form of Sankara (Siva) and Nārāyana (Vishnu). The illustration given (fig. 81) comes from Nāmakkal. A similar but more finished figure of Sankaranārāyana is found at Chidambaram in which attendant sages and demi-gods are also depicted.

HARIHARA OR SANKARA-NĀRAYANA.

XVI

Fine images of Siva represented as the slayer of the elephant-demon are not uncommon in South-Indian temples. In this form he receives the name Gajahāmūrti. The image has eight hands generally, but may have occasionally only four. The two uppermost hands are stretched out and hold the hide of the elephant with its tail bent upwards in the form of an aureola, while on the sides of this aureola are seen .the legs of the elephant hanging. In the three right hands are held the trident, the kettle-drum (or the sword) and the noose (or the tusk of the elephant). Two of the three left hands hold the tusk (or shield) and the skull *(kapāla)*, while the third exhibits the posture indicating astonishment *(vismaya)* or sometimes holds a bell. The left leg is placed on the elephant-head of the giant and the right is raised up so as to reach the left thigh. A good figure answering to this description comes from Pērūr near Coimbatore. The Valuvūr image (Madras Archæological Survey Report for 1911-12, Plate IX, fig. 2) and the Tirutturaippūndi and the Dhārāsuram images (here illustrated) show the contrary position of the legs. The god has a terrible face with protruding teeth; and by his side is seen standing the

GAJAHĀ MŪRTI.

FIG. 79.—Ardhanāri; Dhārāsuram.

FIG. 80.—Ardhanâri ; Tiruvâdi.

FIG. 81.—Sankaranārāyana ; Nāmakkal.

frightened goddess Umā with the young Skanda beside her (fig. 82). The *Kāraṇāgama* mentions the weapons *tanka* and deer and the pointing-finger-pose *(sūchi)*.[1] This last posture of the hand is noticed both in the Tirutturaippūndi and the Dhārāsuram stone images. The former has perhaps five heads (of which three alone are visible on the picture). It has ten hands and more attendant figures (fig. 83).

XVII

GANGĀDHARA

Gangādhara, "the bearer of Ganga (the Ganges)," is a form of Siva which illustrates a well-known *Purānic* story. The story of the descent of the heavenly Ganges into the earth to purify the ashes of the sinful sons of Sagara, a king of the Solar race, is related in the *Rāmāyana*. At the prayer of Bhagīratha, a later member of the same family, "the river of the gods" consented to direct her course to the earth, but her force was such that the earth was unable to bear the shock. So Bhagīratha prayed to Siva and the latter consented to receive the Ganges on his matted locks. The river, proud of her might, came down with all her force as if to crush Siva, but found herself lost altogether in the tangled maze of Siva's locks. Ganga then became humble and Siva let her flow forth again from his locks in a tiny trickle. The river-goddess, the heavenly Ganges, is believed since then to abide in Siva's matted hair as one of his consorts. This latter subject of letting the Ganges flow out of his matted hair as a tiny rivulet is represented in figures generally known as Gangāvisarjanamūrti. No distinction, however, has been made in the *Āgamas* between Gangādhara and Gangāvisarjana. He stands on a lotus pedestal with the right leg straight and the left slightly bent. The image is represented as embracing the goddess Gaurī, consoling and assuring her that his affections would not be transferred to the river-goddess.[2] One right arm holds up a lock of his hair, on which is seen the goddess Gangā. A left arm holds the antelope. The goddess Gaurī with a dejected face *(virahitānanā)* is represented in the *samabhanga* posture with her left leg placed straight on the pedestal and the right leg slightly bent. Her right hand stretches down or is sometimes held

GANGĀVISARJANAMŪRTI.

---

[1] The *Silparatna* defines this as a pose of hand in which the second finger *(tarjani)* is kept straight while the others are bent inwards. It is also adopted when images are made to hold the goad or other similar weapons.

[2] The *Silpasangraha* says that the right lower arm of Siva may be in the posture of giving boons. The illustrations, however, show it holding the face of the goddess Gaurī.

FIG. 82.—Gajahāmūrti; Dhārāsuram.

FIG. 83.—Gajahāmūrti ; Tirutturaippūndi.

akimbo while the left holds a flower. The god and the goddess are highly decorated (figs. 84 and 85). In the first illustration from Gangaikondasōlapuram, Gaurī appears as if she is desirous of being let alone but her anxious husband is holding her fast. Figures of Gangādhara are sometimes seen without Gaurī on the side. In such cases he has four hands, of which the right upper supports Gangā on the lock and the left upper holds the deer. Of the two others the right fore-arm rests on the face of the bull against which the god leans and the left rests freely on the waist (fig. 86). The bull, not seen in the illustration, is distinct in a similar figure from the Siva temple at Kodumbālūr. Bhagīratha, who was the cause of the descent of Gangā, may also be shown standing together with other *rishis* to the right of Siva. This is found only in an illustration from Burgess's *Elura Cave Temples.*[1]

One other figure (or rather group of figures) representing Gangādhara (fig. 87) comes from the rock-cut cave at Trichinopoly and deserves notice. The central image is Siva with four hands. The upper right hand holds a lock of hair in order to receive evidently the goddess Gangā descending from the clouds. The upper left seems to hold a rosary. The left lower hand rests on the waist and the corresponding right holds by the tail a serpent with the raised hood. The left leg of Siva is placed straight on the ground and the right which is bent at the knee is placed on the head of a demon (perhaps Musalagan) who also supports the leg with his left hand which is raised up. The god is fully decorated. Round him are four attendant sages, two of whom are kneeling at the feet, the other two worshipping from behind. Above the group are two *dēvas* flying in the air on either side of the god's head. Although the details given above do not agree with any particular description given in the *Āgamas,* it appears to me that it represents Siva standing ready prepared to receive in his locks the rushing torrent of the river of the gods. One of the attendant sages may, in this case, be Bhagīratha at whose request Gangā descended from the heavens.

XVIII

KĀLAHARA-MŪRTI.

Another *Purānic* story is illustrated in the form Kālahā, or Kālaharamūrti, "the destroyer of the god of Death." Mārkandēya was a young boy, greatly devoted to the worship of Siva. The fates had decreed that he should not live

[1] Plate XLIII, fig. 1, and Plate XXVI, fig. 1.

FIG. 84.—Gangādhara ; Gangaikondasōlapuram.

FIG. 85.- Gangádhara (metal); Vaidîsvarankōyil.

FIG. 86.—Gangādhara ; Tanjore.

FIG. 87.—Gangādharam ; Trichinopoly.

beyond his sixteenth year. His father was very disconsolate as the boy approached the end of his appointed time on earth. But Mārkandēya was not afraid and spent all his time worshipping Siva. While thus engaged, the god of Death (Kāla), whose duty it is to take the breath of life away from the mortal body at the appointed time, came up to the boy, with his weapons, the club and the noose, riding on his fierce buffalo. He was not daunted by the fact that the boy was engaged in holy duty but at once threw his relentless noose on the boy and began to pull his life out. The boy was frightened at the sight of the terrible god of Death and caught hold of the Siva-*linga* with both his hands. Siva then burst out from within the *linga* and, with one foot still placed on the *linga*, he kicked with the other the transgressing god of Death, pierced him with his trident and vanquished him.[1] This is the *Purānic* story of Kālaharamūrti. According to the *Āgamas* he is represented as placing his right leg on the *linga* in the same attitude as that of the dancing Natarāja. His left leg, which is bent and raised, is placed on the breast of Kāla. The god wears a *jatāmakuta* and has an angry look, protruding teeth, three eyes and four (or sometimes eight) hands. The fore-arm on the right side holds the trident pointed downwards and raised to the level of the ear. The other right hand holds the axe while the two left hands exhibit the *varada* (with skull in palm) and the *vismaya*[2] postures (fig. 88). The *Kāranāgama* adds that he must also be accompanied by the goddess. The god of Death has two arms and protruding teeth. He holds the noose and is lying flat on the ground with legs stretched out wide apart. In the sketch from Chandragiri (fig. 89) is seen Mārkandēya with the noose round his neck and embracing the *linga*. Siva also is seen holding the trident in two hands while Yama is attacking the young sage with a trident.

XIX

Nīlakantha or Srīkantha.

Nīlakantha, Srīkantha and Vishakantha are three synonymous names of Siva, given to him on account of his having swallowed the deadly poison *(kālakūta)* produced at the churning of the ocean by the *dēvas* and *dānavas* under instructions from the Creator, in order to obtain divine nectar. The

---

1 See Burgess's *Elura Cave Temples*, Plate XXIV.

2 In place of the *varada* some figures show the *sūchi* and in place of the *vismaya*, the hand holding the deer. According to the *Silpasangraha* the symbols may be the trident and the kettle-drum in the right hands and the boon-giving posture and the axe in the left.

FIG. 88.—Kālahāramūrti; Paṭṭīsvaram.

Fig. 89.—Kālaharamūrti; Chandragiri.

mountain Mandara was their churn-stick, the primeval Tortoise (who was Vishnu himself) the pivot on which the stick rested and turned, and the serpent Vāsuki the churning rope. By a clever device of Vishnu, the *dānavas* held the head and the *dēvas* the tail of the serpent. They churned and churned. Many great and splendid things came foaming up and every one was eager to seize what pleased him most. But all at once something black began to rise. It grew and grew and darkened the whole universe. All the gods and demons were mortally afraid. For it was the deadliest of poisons, death to them and death to all the universe. In this moment of horror they called on Siva to help them. The mighty god came and took the poison in the hollow of his hand and swallowed it. That which was enough to kill the universe served only to stain his neck with a bluish tint. Thus he came to be called "the poison-necked" or "the blue-necked" god.[1] The *Kāranāgama* describing a form of Siva called

VISHĀPAHARAMŪRTI.

Vishāpaharamūrti, "the destroyer of poison" says that he has one face, three eyes, braided hair and four arms holding in the two upper the antelope and the axe. He is in the posture of drinking the poison which is held in the right lower hand. The left lower shows the boon-giving posture. On the left side of the god is the goddess with two arms. She shows an anxious countenance and holds the neck of Siva as if to prevent the poison from going down.

XX

TRIPURĀNTAKAMŪRTI.

Two other forms of Siva connected with *Purānic* stories may be mentioned. These are Tripurāntakamūrti and Kirātārjunamūrti. The first was assumed by Siva when he killed the three demons called Tripura and reduced their three magic cities to ashes. During this campaign the Earth is said to have served Siva as a chariot, and the Sun and the Moon as its wheels. The four Vēdas were the four horses and the Upanishads were the guiding reins; the mythic golden mountain Mēru was the bow, the ocean was the quiver and god Vishnu was the arrow. Images of Tripurāntaka are made with the right leg firmly placed on the pedestal and the left leg bent. The right fore-hand in the *simha-karna* posture holds the arrow and the left fore-arm, the bow. The other hands hold the *tanka* (or the

---

[1] The *Kāsyapa-Silpa* speaking of Srīkantha says that he holds the trident and the kettle-drum.

[2] An image of Tripurāntaka in the thousand-pillared hall of the Madura temple shows an actual figure of Vishnu engraved on the arrow held by Siva.

axe) and the deer respectively. The locks are arranged in the form of a *jatāmakuta* and the goddess Gaurī stands on the left side. The accompanying illustration from Chidambaram (fig. 90) answers to this description of Tripurāntaka. The alternating positions of the leg, the existence or non-existence of the demon Apasmāra underneath one of them and the fashion of holding the bow and the arrow, yield five other forms of Tripurāntaka, who may also be represented with eight or ten arms. Sometimes (when with ten arms), the god is seated in a chariot with his right knee touching the *sudhā*, the left leg which is bent at the knee being placed firmly in front of the right. In the chariot, at its front, is seated the four-faced Brahmā and below him is a white bull drawing the car. A sandal-wood carving published in the *Journal of Indian Art and Industry*, Vol. XV, No. 119, fig. 12, shows the actual fight between Siva and the demon called Tripura.

Kirātārjunamūrti.

Kirātārjunamūrti is that form of Siva in which he is supposed to have appeared before Arjuna, one of the heroes of the epic *Mahābhārata*, when the latter was doing penance to obtain from Siva a powerful weapon with which he could destroy his enemies. God Siva wished to try personally if his devotee Arjuna really deserved to wield the matchless weapon *Pāsupata*, whose presiding deity was himself. To this end Siva and Pārvatī assumed the forms of a hunter and a huntress and with their retinue of demons and hobgoblins attired for the chase, drove before them a wild boar, which rushed to attack Arjuna who was then performing his penance. Arjuna, the practised warrior, seized his bow and instantly shot the animal. Simultaneously also came another arrow from the psuedo-hunter Siva. Pierced by both the arrows, the animal died. The hunter cried out that the quarry was his and asked Arjuna how he dared to shoot at it. The royal hero of the Lunar race could not brook the insult from this wild hunter of the woods. A fierce fight between the two was the result. Arjuna was amazed to see that the hunter was more than his match. Arjuna's never failing arrows failed him now and he challenged the hunter to a hand-to-hand contest. Sore and beaten, Arjuna worshipped the clay *linga* of the god Siva that he had before him, when, lo! the flowers he threw on the *linga* fell on the person of the hunter. Arjuna struck the hunter at the head with his powerful bow called *Gāndiva* and drew blood. But the bow was mysteriously snatched away from him. In the end Arjuna was overcome by a gentle touch of the mighty god. Arjuna then knew him and begged pardon and the god gave him the desired weapon *Pāsupata*.

FIG. 90.—Tripurântakamûrti ; Chidambaram.

This story is the subject matter of the exquisite poem *Kirātārjuniya* of the Sanskrit poet Bhāravi. The Tanjore inscriptions refer to an image Kirātārjunadēva;[1] and from the description given of it in a mutilated passage, it appears as if there was a reference there, to a *linga* or to some object connected with it. Images of Kirātārjunamūrti answering to the story described above are not very frequent. An illustration (fig. 91) which comes from Pushpagiri in the Cuddapah district represents evidently the last part of the drama, when Siva and Pārvatī appeared before Arjuna and gave him the weapon. Siva holds in his back hands the axe and the trident. In his right fore-arm is the arrow *Pāsupata*, the left fore-arm resting freely on the waist. To the left of Siva stands the goddess Pārvatī with two hands, holding a lotus flower in her right. In front of both, is Arjuna in the modest posture of receiving with both hands the divine gift offered him. A pigmy figure standing between Siva and Arjuna in the illustration may be one of the attendants of Siva. The *Kāranāgama* gives the same description but makes Siva wear both the arrow and the bow and hold the antelope instead of the trident. An illustration coming from Chidambaram (fig. 92) answers to this description. In it may also be seen the figure of Arjuna in a worshipping posture as described in the *Kāranāgama*. It may be noted that the historic "Arjuna's Penance" at Mahābalipuram is supposed to represent the *Mahābhārata* story related above.[2]

XXI

CHANDĒSĀNUGRAHAMŪRTI.

Chandēsānugrahamūrti is a form of Siva which was assumed by him in order to confer blessings on his fervent devotee Chandēsa described in the sequel.[3] His figures are occasionally found depicted in some of the South-Indian temples. From Gangaikondasōlapuram in the Trichinopoly district comes a beautiful illustration (fig. 93) of the story.

1 Dr. Ananda K. Coomaraswami publishes an image of Siva from Tanjore in his Art Journal *Visvakarma* (Part II, No. 28). In this the positions of the four hands indicate the nature of the weapons that must have been held by them. Although the image is called Gangādhara by Dr. Coomaraswami, the poses of the fingers suggest that the image must be one of Kirātārjuna, possibly the very idol mentioned in the Tanjore inscriptions, since its two fore-arms are so adjusted as to receive into them the bow and the arrow. The upper arms in this case must have held the axe and the deer. Mr. R. D. Banerji describes in the Director-General's *Archæological Survey Report* for 1911-12, pp. 161 ff., certain sculptures from Chandimau which relate to this story of Arjuna's fight with Siva. These are attributed by Mr. Banerji to the Gupta period.

2 Havell's *Ideals of Indian Art*, pp. 147 to 151.

3 See p. 161, below.

FIG. 91.—Kirātārjunamūrti ; Pushpagiri.

FIG. 92 —Kirātārjunamūrti; Chidambaram.

FIG. 93.—Chaṇḍēśānugrahamūrti ; Gangaikondasōlapuram.

Here Siva is seated in the *sukhāsana* or the comfortable posture on a raised pedestal, as in the case of Sōmāskanda figures, his left leg hanging down and resting on a foot-stool. The goddess Pārvatī too is seated to the left of Siva on the same pedestal, her right leg being bent at the knee and placed on the pedestal while the left is hanging down to rest on another foot-stool. Siva has four arms. In his two back hands he holds the axe and the deer and with the two front arms he is seen decorating with a flower garland the locks of his servant, the devoted Chandēsa. The latter sits on the ground at the foot of Siva, with bending knees and folded arms, and receives the divine favour with gratitude. The images are well ornamented. Above the group are seen flying gods and demi-gods who have evidently gathered round to see the kindness of Siva shown towards his devotee. According to the *Mayamata* Chandēsa has behind his folded arms the weapon *parasu* (axe). On the east *gōpura* of the Chidambaram temple is a figure of Chandēsānugrahamūrti in which Chandēsa is represented with the axe between his folded arms.

The size of the image of Chandēsa must, it is stated, be small so as to reach the arms of Siva and is to be bedecked with the ornaments of children. The *Kāsyapa-Silpa* states that between the god and the goddess may be placed the figure of Skanda, at the sculptor's option. "Next to Dakshināmūrti," it says, "the figure of Chandēsānugraha is the most famous." A group of images under the name Chandēsvaraprasādadēva was set up in the Tanjore temple by king Rājarāja I, and consisted of (1) the god Chandēsvaraprasādadēva with four arms, (2) the demon Musalagan with two arms, (3) the goddess Umāparamēsvarī, (4) Mahādēva (the *linga* worshipped evidently by the boy Chandēsa), (5) the devotee with two arms, (6) his father also with two arms represented as having fallen down and lying on the ground and (7) Chandēsa receiving with his two arms the boon of a flower-garland from Siva.[1] This description agrees with the story related in the *Periyapurānam*, a compilation of the thirteenth century A.D. The *Kāranāgama,* whose date is not known, was also apparently familiar with the story.

XXII

Some particularly fierce forms of Siva may now be described. First in fierceness comes the form of the fabulous SARABHA-MŪRTI.

1 *South-Indian Inscriptions*, Vol. II, Introduction, p. 39.

Sarabha which is supposed to have been assumed by Siva in order to suppress the pride of Narasimha, the Man-lion incarnation of Vishnu. The *Kāranāgama* describes Sarabha as having eight legs, three eyes, long nails, two hands and a body glowing like fire. The image has a lion's face and two wings one of which is said to represent the fierce goddess Durgā and the other, Death.[1] The illustration here reproduced (fig. 94) shows Sarabha trampling on the Man-lion.

PĀSUPATA-MŪRTI.

Pāsupatamūrti is another fierce form of Siva. This is evidently the form in which he is worshipped by the sect of Pāsupata Saivas, who, according to Dr. Bhandarkar, came into prominence about the second century B.C.[2] The *Silpasāra* describes Pāsupatamūrti as having ten arms and five faces. According to other *Agamas* the figure may have only four arms. It has a fierce face, knitted brows over its three eyes, and hair red like flames of fire, bristling erect on the head. The god holds in his right hand a trident pointing downwards and in the boon-giving palm of the left he also holds a skull *(kapāla)*. Sometimes the handle of the trident is lightly held by both the lower arms, which do not then show the *varada* and the *abhaya* postures. In the back arms are seen the *tanka* and the sword. The protruding teeth and the sacred thread formed of a venomous serpent add to the fierceness of his appearance. For purposes of meditation, however, a milder form is adopted, in which, like Chandrasēkhara, the god is represented standing or seated with a smiling countenance, showing the trident and the *abhaya* in his two right arms and the rosary and the *varada* in the two left arms (fig. 95).

RAKSHŌ-GHNAMŪRTI.

Two other terrible forms of Siva are Aghōramūrti and Rakshōghnamūrti. The latter has braided hair and a body besmeared with ashes. In one hand he holds a trident with which he is piercing the god Yama, who calls away unto him the victims of all cruel diseases. In another hand is a skull from which issues a blazing fire. The axe and the kettle-drum are other weapons held by him. With his formidable projecting teeth, knitted eyebrows and frowning face he is represented as feasting on corpses in the company of *bhūtas*, *prētas* and *pisāchas* in the burning ground, which is his usual dwelling place. I have not, however, seen any actual representation of this image in South-Indian temples.

AGHŌRA-MŪRTI.

Aghōramūrti has four faces and eight hands. In these he holds the *kuthāra* (axe), Vēdas, noose, goad, kettle-drum, rosary, trident

---

[1] Madras Archæological Survey Report for 1911-12, Plate IX, Fig. 1.

[2] *Vaishanavism, Sivism*, etc., p. 116 f.

FIG. 94.—Sarabhamūrti; Dhārāsuram.

Fig. 95.—Pāsupatamūrti ; Chidambaram.

and the skull. He has terrible protruding teeth and a dark shining body (fig. 96). The *Sivatattvaratnākara* mentions a form of Aghōramūrti with thirty-two arms and the *Pāncharātrāgama,* another with twelve arms. The image wears a garland of skulls and treads on the head of Kālamunda, the vile god of Death.

Bhairava, born of the blood of Siva, is another god of this class. The *Tantrasāra* mentions eight forms of Bhairava which are fit for worship. His general form shows dishevelled matted hair, three eyes and a red-coloured body. His symbols are the trident, sword, noose and the kettle-drum. He is naked and is represented as being followed by all kinds of demons and spirits and riding on a dog (fig. 97). Hēmādri describes Bhairava as a pot-bellied god with round red eyes, terrible face, protruding teeth and wide nostrils. He wears a garland of skulls and ornaments of snakes,[1] thus frightening even his consort who stands by his side. The upper half of his body which is dark in colour is covered with the elephant's hide. He has many arms and holds all destructive weapons. The *Silpasāra* makes him seated on a jewelled throne under the celestial tree *mandāra,* closely embraced by the goddess. The same work mentions three other forms of Bhairava, viz., Panchavaktra-Bhairava, Gōvinda-Bhairava and Samhāra-Bhairava. The second of these has four arms and holds the conch, discus, drinking cup and the mace. He has three eyes and is young, serene and naked. On his side is the goddess Vaishnavī-Sakti and his vehicle is the bird Garuda. The third has five faces and ten arms and among his weapons are also the Vaishnavite conch and discus.

BHAIRAVA.

GŌVINDA-BHAIRAVA. SAMHĀRA-BHAIRAVA.

According to the *Silpasāra* Kāla-Bhairava wears a girdle of tiny bells on his waist and holds the sword, trident, drum and the drinking cup in his hands. He has a fearsome face with protruding teeth, a garland of skulls and dishevelled hair. In the illustration from Durgi (fig. 98) the dog which is his vehicle is seen biting a human head held by the left lower hand of the image. The goddess with her companion is standing to the right, evidently frightened at the serpent ornaments and the terrible form of Bhairava.

KĀLA-BHAIRAVA.

Mahākāla, still another fierce form of Siva, is quite like Bhairava, but holds a serpent in the place of the noose. In the work entitled *Lalitōpākhyāna* he is described as accompanied by Kālī, embracing her and drinking with her "from

MAHĀKĀLA

[1] Figures of Bhairava with the dog vehicle and the five-hooded serpent overhead, are reported to exist in some of the ancient temples of the Bellary district.

FIG. 96.- Agōhramūrti ; Paṭṭīsvaram.

FIG. 97.—Bhairava ; Pattisvaram.

FIG. 98.—Kāla-Bhairava ; Durgi.

the cup which is the mundane egg, the wine which is the essence of creation." His faces (evidently five) are terrible to look at, like those of death, and threaten to swallow the universe.

Kālāgni-Rudra "the terrible or fiery Rudra" described in the *Kāsyapa-Silpa*, closely resembles Bhairava and is perhaps only another form of him.[1] He holds the weapons sword and shield, the arrow and the bow and wears a red cloth. The illustration from Durgi (fig. 99) is very likely one of Kālāgni-Rudra. KĀLĀGNI-RUDRA.

XXIII

Vīrabhadra is one of the many Saiva demi-gods *(ganas)*.[2] VĪRABHADRA. He is said to have sprung from a lock of Siva's hair when, as already stated, Siva heard of the suicide of his wife Satī in her father's sacrificial fire and flew into a rage. From the fire of his anger came into existence this terrible form, as of Death manifest, who destroyed the sacrificial ceremonies of Daksha and slew Daksha himself. The *Pāncharātrāgama* describes Vīrabhadra as black in colour, having three eyes and holding in his four arms a sword, arrow, bow and club. He wears a garland of skulls and has sandals on his feet. A yellow garment is tied round his loins.[3] The *Silparatna* describes him as having eight hands and riding on *vētāla* (a demon) surrounded by his *ganas* (followers). From the Brihadīsvara temple at Tanjore comes a sculptured panel (fig. 100) in which a woman, perhaps the wife of Daksha, is seen flying in alarm with upraised hands at seeing her husband decapitated by Vīrabhadra before her very eyes and the severed head thrown into the sacrificial fire-pit. One of the attendant priests with a ladle in his hand is also represented in the act of running away from the scene. A fine figure of Vīrabhadra with the bow and arrow, sword and shield, comes from Mudigondam in the Coimbatore district (fig. 101). The god is represented standing on a *padma-pītha* in front of a *prabhā-mandala*, "an arch of light". At the edge of the pedestal on the right side is shown Daksha who was, however, revived by Siva with the head of a sheep substituted for the one that was burnt in the sacrificial fire.

[1] The *Rudrayāmala-Tantra* includes the name Kālāgni-Rudra among the 64 varieties of Bhairava.

[2] *Kāsikhanda*. In the lexicon *Amarakōsa* Siva himself is called the destroyer of the sacrifice (Kratudhvamsin).

[3] The *Kāranāgama* adds that he has Bhadrakālī by his side and is fierce. Daksha with the sheep's head, two eyes and two arms, stands on the right side of Vīrabhadra.

FIG. 99.—Kālāgni-Rudra (?) ; Durgi.

FIG. 100.—Vīrabhadra throwing the head of Daksha into the fire ; Tanjore.

FIG. 101.—Vīrabhadra ; Mudigondam.

The figure of Daksha is of comparatively small stature, meant evidently to indicate by contrast, the huge form of Vīrabhadra.

The *Silpasangraha* mentions three varieties of Vīrabhadra (viz. *sāttvic, tāmasic* and *rājasic)* with two, four or eight arms.[1] All are dark in colour and fierce looking. Seated figures of Vīrabhadra are called Yōga-Vīra, his standing figures, Bhōga-Vīra and those in a walking posture, Vīra-Vīra. In the first, Vīrabhadra holds a sword and shield and is seated with one leg folded on the pedestal and the other hanging down. In the second posture he exhibits the bow and arrow, sword and *kataka.* On the leg is worn the anklet of heroes. The head is adorned with a crown, in the middle of which is represented a *linga.* A garland of skulls decorates the neck. On the right side is the image of Daksha with folded arms. In the Vīra-Vīra figures, Vīrabhadra holds the trident, sword, arrow and the deer on the right side and the skull, shield, bow and the goad on the left. It may be noted that, while images of Vīrabhadra and independent temples erected for him are very common in the Telugu and Canarese districts, temples in the Tamil districts rarely contain his image, and shrines dedicated to him are still rarer. There is a Vīrabhadra temple at Madura,

XXIV

Images of Kshētrapāla often met with in the temples of Southern India are divided into three classes, according to the predominating qualities *sattva, rajas* and *tamas.* Those belonging to the first class have two or four hands; the second six and the third eight.[2] All the figures, irrespective of the class to which they belong, are made to stand with level feet *(samapāda).* The general description of them is that they have three eyes which are round and protruding, red hair pointing upwards, serpent jewels, a girdle of bells round the waist and a necklace of skulls. They are naked and inspire awe with their fierce fangs (fig. 102). Kshētrapāla occupies an important place among the subsidiary deities in Siva temples. He is the chief guardian of the temple just as Chandēsa (described below) is its superintendent and

KSHĒTRA-PĀLA.

[1] Dr. Burgess's *Elura Cave Temples,* Plate XXII, Fig. 2, is a representation of Vīrabhadra with eight hands. The plate wrongly calls the figure Bhairava.

[2] One image of Kshētrapāla with eight arms and another of Bhairava, were set up in the Tanjore temple at the beginning of the eleventh century A.D. in connexion with the group of figures illustrating the story of the Saiva saint Siruttonda-Nāyanār; see below, p. 259, footnote 2. In the Panchanadēsvara temple at Tiruvādi near Tanjore is an image of Kshētrapāla, called Ālkondār, with eight hands, to which people attach much importance.

FIG. 102.—Kshētrapāla; Tiruvarangulam.

manager. Kshētrapāla is worshipped first in every Siva temple, before commencing the regular service for the day. The *Prayōgasāra* says :—" Whoever performs any ceremony without first worshipping Kshētrapāla, the fruit of that ceremony is without doubt destroyed by Kshētrapāla." His naked form and the name Mahā-Bhairava by which he is addressed during the *Sribali* ceremony suggests that Kshētrapāla in his essence must be allied to Bhairava.[1]

All these awe-inspiring forms of the Saiva cult, including others which are mentioned in the *Āgamas*, but not often met with in South-Indian temples, received special worship from the adherents of the early Saiva sub-sects known as Pāsupatas, Kālāmukhas and Kāpalikas, as well as from the Lingāyatas of later origin.[2]

XXV

Among the attendant *ganas* of Siva who, like the gods just described, are identified with one or another aspect of Siva himself, may be mentioned Chandēsa, Bhringīsa and Nandīsa. The first is counted as the foremost of the servants of Siva and is hence called in Tamil inscriptions and the *Periyapurānam*, Ādidāsa-Chandēsa.[3] The *Kāsyapa-Silpa* tells us that he is made up of the sterner side of Siva's nature and appears in each millennium *(yuga)* with different names and symbols. In the Krita-yuga he receives the name Prachanda, is of angry appearance, rides on an elephant and has the *jatāmakuta* and sixteen arms. In Trētā-yuga he is seen smiling, has eight arms and dishevelled braids of hair, and goes by the name Chanda. In the third or Dvāpara-yuga he has four hands, the lion vehicle, *jatāmandala*, protruding teeth and a fearful face. His weapons then are the *tanka*, trident, noose and the hook. In the Kali-yuga he has a peaceful appearance and the bull vehicle, has his locks made up in the

CHANDĒSA.

[1] *Mayūrabhanja*, (p. xxxiv, fig. 13), gives a description of Kshētrapāla calling him Mahākāla and Bhairava. The *Silpasāra* in describing Vatuka-Bhairava, calls him also Kshētrapāla.

[2] In the famous temple on the Srīsailam Hill (Kurnool district) where the influence of the Lingāyata sect was once very great, is a pavilion adjoining the Nandi-*mandapa*. An inscription of the fourteenth century A.D. describes it as the place where the votaries, evidently of the Vīrabhadra form of Siva, offered up their heads in order to propitiate the furious god; Madras Epigraphical Report for 1914-15, p. 92, paragraph 15.

[3] In Epigraphic records the documentary transactions of a Siva temple are stated to be conducted in the name of Chandēsa, the supposed manager of the temple. Even now, visitors to a Siva shrine have to report themselves before Chandēsa prior to leaving the temple premises and clap their hands as if to show that they are not carrying with them any portion of the temple property.

form of either a *jatāmakuta, jatāmandala* or *kēsabandha* and stands with level feet in the *ābhanga* or the *sama-bhanga* posture. He may also be found seated with the right leg hanging down from the seat and the left leg bent crosswise so as to rest upon the seat. He holds the *tanka* (or, axe) in the right hand and shows the boon-giving posture in his left (fig. 103).[1] Sometimes both the hands are seen folded over the breast in a worshipping posture with the weapon *tanka* (or, sometimes, a flower garland) held between them. In this case he receives the name Ādi-Chandēsa. A story related in the Tamil *Periyapurānam* about Chandēsa makes him a fervent devotee of Siva, who in his height of devotion, cut off the legs of his own father, because he wantonly spilt the milk-pots which Chandēsa had secured as loving offerings to Siva. Sankarāchārya, who lived perhaps in the early part of the eighth century A.D., refers to this Saiva devotee Chandēsa as *pitridrōhin*, "the sinner against (his) father," evidently with reference to the story related in the *Periyapurānam*. The form of Siva known as Chandēsānugrahamūrti, described above, is entirely based on this anecdote.

NANDĪSA. Nandi, Nandīsa or Nandikēsvara, now represented by the recumbent bull placed in front of the chief shrine in a Siva temple, is described by Hēmādri to be one of the attendant demi-gods of Siva. He is stated to have three eyes and four arms and to wear a tiger's skin. In two of his hands he holds the trident and the *bhindivāla* "a short javelin." The third hand is raised up over the head and the last shows a stretched finger *(tarjanī)*, his eyes being watchful and fixed towards people coming from a distance into the Siva temple. The Varāha-*Purāna* says that, though originally an ascetic, Nandi by his austerities and devotion to Siva was blessed with a form similar to that of Siva himself and was placed at the head of the attendant *ganas* of Siva. A metallic image (fig. 104) from Valuvūr (Tanjore district) represents him in this metamorphosed form. He has four arms of which the two back ones hold the *tanka* and the deer and the two front are joined together palm to palm in a worshipping posture. By the side of Nandīsvara stands also his wife with two arms.[2]

---

[1] This last is the form of Chandēsa usually found in Siva temples. In the illustration, however, the left hand rests on the thigh and the position of the legs is reversed.

[2] A verse in praise of Nandi describes him as the husband of Suyasā. He stands at the entrance into Siva temples with a knife or golden cane held in his hands so as to touch the *kūrpara* of his right arm. In one of the *mandapas* of the Ēkāmrēsvara temple at Conjeeveram, Nandi is represented in the same posture as Garuda, carrying in his out-stretched fore-arms the feet of Siva and Pārvatī.

FIG. 103.—Chandèsa ; Tiruvottiyūr.

FIG. 104.—Nandisa and his consort (metal); Valuvūr.

It must be noted that Nandīsa is a favourite deity of the Saiva puritans, the so-called Lingāyatas or Vīra-Saivas.

Bhringi, Bhringiriti or Bhringīsa is similarly a fervent devotee of Siva. So exclusive was he in his devotion that he is said to have ignored the goddess who was part and parcel of Siva. His sole business in life, to which he had pledged himself, was ever to circumambulate the *linga* of Siva and no one else. To test his faith the god assumed the hermaphrodite form of Ardhanāri in which the goddess, as already described, is not separated from the god. Bhringi was not baffled; but assuming the form of a bee *(bhringa)* he bored into the united body and continued still to go round and round the Siva half of the hermaphrodite. The goddess Pārvatī was enraged and cursed him to become emaciated day after day. Bhringi, accordingly, grew very thin and was unable to support himself. With the grace of Siva he secured a third leg which supported him. Thus Bhringi is represented in pictures with three legs (fig. 105).[1] An image of Bhringīsa with three arms and three legs is stated to have been set up in the temple at Tanjore by a subordinate of Rājarāja I in the eleventh century A.D. BHRINGĪSA.

Jvaradēva of Saiva mythology, who is supposed to have been the destroyer of the demon Bhasmāsura, is described in the *Āgamas* as having three legs, three heads, six arms, nine eyes, and a dejected appearance. An image from Bhavāni in the Coimbatore district (fig. 106) answers to this description of Jvaradēva. JVARADĒVA.

XXVI

Ganapati, Ganēsa or Vināyaka, the popular "belly god," is, as his name indicates, the chief of the Saiva *gaṇas*. He is said to be the eldest son of Siva and Pārvatī, to have three eyes, an elephant's head[2] and ears and four arms. In the GANAPATI, GANĒSA OR VINĀYAKA.

[1] The Vāmana-*Purāna* states that Bhringi was the name conferred by Siva on the demon Andhaka after the latter had proved himself to be a staunch devotee of Siva. Bhringi is represented with an emaciated body holding the staff in one hand and the rosary in the other. His eyes are ever directed towards Siva.

[2] One of the popular stories explaining how Ganapati came to have the elephant's head is as follows: Once upon a time when Pārvatī went to bathe, she made a figure of the turmeric which had been smeared over her body, gave it life and limbs and appointed it to keep watch at the door. Siva came to see Pārvatī but was stopped at the door by the newly created guard. Siva in anger cut off the head of the figure. The goddess entreated him to revive her child. He agreed and said that the head of any living body sleeping with the head placed northward might be severed at once and placed on the trunk of the turmeric figure. An elephant was found sleeping in the way described. Its head was accordingly cut

FIG. 105.—Bhringi; Srīsailam.

FIG. 106.—Jvaradēva; Bhavāni.

two back hands he holds the hook and the noose and in the front arms an elephant's tusk and the wood-apple. Instead of the two last we may sometimes find the boon-conferring posture and the water-pot. According to the *Kāsyapa-Silpa* the noose may alternate with the rosary or a serpent. The illustration from Lēpākshi (fig. 107) shows the left lower hand of Ganēsa resting on his thigh. His elephant trunk is curved out in the act of picking up the wood-apple or, sometimes, the pudding. His pot-belly is girded round by a serpent and the sacred thread, which is also a serpent, hangs across the body from over his left shoulder. In the seated posture Ganēsa is represented with one leg hanging from the pedestal and placed on a foot-stool and the other resting on the pedestal. The right tusk of the god is broken and must in no case be shown complete.[1] He rides on a rat or bandicoot. His image may be made standing (fig. 108), seated (fig. 109) or dancing (fig. 110).[2] In the first position the general bend of the body known as *ābhanga* or *samabhanga* may optionally be adopted. While seated, the body is to be slightly bent to the left. Over his head Ganēsa wears the jewelled crown *(kiritamakuta)* and his hands and legs are fully ornamented.

Ganapati is a very important deity in the Hindu Pantheon.[3] Supposed to be the lord of obstacles (Vighnēsvara) he is worshipped by all classes of Hindus, other than Srī-Vaishnavas, at the commencement of every religious ceremony, whether auspicious or inauspicious. A sect of Brahmanas called Gānāpatyas, found mostly on the West Coast, worship him as the highest of the gods. As in the case of Vishnu and Siva he is

off and placed on the trunk. The figure came back to life and Siva accepting that as his first-born child, blessed him and made him the leader *(pati)* of the Saiva hosts *(ganas)*. People still believe that it is not right to sleep with one's head placed northward. The Brahmavaivarta-*Purāna* gives a different account and makes Vishnu responsible for the change in Ganapati's head.

[1] In the *Sukranitisāra* it is stated that his left *(vāma)* tusk is broken, that his vehicle may be any animal which he chooses and that his trunk holds a lotus.

[2] The dancing figure of Ganēsa from Gangaikondasōlapuram has its upper left hand lifted up instead of showing the noose or the rosary.

[3] Babu Nagendra Natha Vasu in his *Mayūrabhanja* states that Vināyaka is worshipped even by the Buddhists, the Japanese calling him Binayakia. He refers to a temple of Ganēsa in Nepal which is supposed to have been built by a daughter of the Maurya king Asōka in the third century B.C. Dr. Bhandarkar (*Vaishnavism, Saivism*, etc., p. 147 f.) gives the sixth century to be the earliest date when Ganapati as the elephant-headed god, came to be generally worshipped by the Hindus.

FIG. 107.—Ganapati standing ; Lēpākshi.

FIG. 108.—Ganapati standing (metal); Pattisvaram.

FIG. 109.—Ganapati seated; Siyamangalam.

FIG. 110.—Ganapati dancing; Gangaikondasōlapuram.

also called by a thousand names. Mr. Havell explains Ganapati to be the *manas*, or worldly wisdom, personified. Ganapati in Hindu mythology is recognized as an unmarried god—a *brahmachārin*. But from the sequel it will appear that some forms of Ganapati have their accompanying goddesses, sometimes, recognized as Ashta-Siddhis (the eight presiding deities of success or achievement).

Thirty-two forms of Ganapati[1] are mentioned in the Mudgala-*Purāna*. The *Silpasāra* also refers to some of these forms. Mahā-Ganapati is stated in the Mudgala-*Purāna* to be an elephant-faced god, three-eyed, wearing the crescent of the moon as his head-ornament, and red in colour. He is lovingly embraced by his wife who, seated on his lap, holds a lotus in her hand. The following weapons and symbols are mentioned: the *bijapūra*, club, sugarcane-bow, a brilliant discus, conch, noose, lotus, ear of paddy, the broken tusk and the ruby-pot. This list indicates that the god must have ten hands.[2] The illustration (fig. 111) from Madura shows Mahā-Ganapati riding on a rat and having on his lap the seated figure of a goddess. He has ten arms but the weapons held in them are not quite distinct. In the uppermost hand on the right side, however, is seen the discus. In the Visvanātha temple at Tenkāsi (Tinnevelly district) we have a similar image seated on a pedestal without the usual rat vehicle, the elephant trunk being turned towards the left side. Here again only the discus and the lotus held in two of the ten arms are clear. Mahā-Ganapati with different weapons and two goddesses receives the name Lakshmī-Ganapati. A fine bronze image of Hēramba-Ganapati, also described in the Mudgala-*Purāna* comes from Negapatam (fig. 112). This figure has five elephant faces, the fifth of which, in the illustration, is represented at the top.[3] Of his ten arms the two lowest show the protecting and the boon-giving postures. The others hold the noose, the tusk, the rosary, hook, axe, pestle, pudding and the fruit. He rides on a lion, but no goddess is found, as in the two varieties just mentioned. From Tiruvānaikkāval (i.e., Jambukēsvaram)

MAHĀ-GANAPATI.

LAKSHMĪ-GANAPATI.

HĒRAMBA-GANAPATI.

---

[1] The *Sāradātilaka* speaks of fifty-one forms of Ganapati.

[2] The *Silparatna* says that he is seated on a lotus-pedestal under a *kalpa*-tree; that he has ten arms holding the weapons mentioned in the Mudgala-*Purāna* and that he is surrounded by gods and *ganas*. No. 84 of the Tanjore inscriptions (*S.I.I.*, Vol. II, p. 407) refers to a comfortably seated Ganapati and mentions a tree as one of his accompaniments. The reference may be to Mahā-Ganapati; but the inscription states that he had only four divine arms.

[3] A stone image of this form of Ganapati is found at Tiruvottiyūr near Madras. It is of recent make and has the five heads all arranged in a circle.

FIG. 111.—Mahā-Gaṇapati ; Madura.

FIG. 112.—Hèramba-Ganapati (metal); Negapatam.

PANCHA-MUKHA-VINĀYAKA.

in the Trichinopoly district, comes a stone figure of Pancha-mukha-Vināyaka which answers to the description of Hēramba-Ganapati without the lion vehicle. There are other forms known as Ūrdhva-Ganapati, Uchchhishta-Ganapati and Vara-Ganapati,[1] which are perhaps the inventions of the followers of that mysterious and often indecent cult of Sāktas, in which the female energy of creation always plays a very prominent part. Sakti-Ganapati and Uddanda-Ganapati are represented as embracing a goddess. Bīja-Ganapati mentioned in the *Silparatna* has four arms, is fond of the citron and is adorned with shining ornaments. Perhaps he is the same as Vijaya-Ganapati of the Mudgala-*Purāna*. It may be noted that in the Brihadīsvara temple at Tanjore, established by the Chōla king Rājarāja I about the beginning of the eleventh century A.D., different forms of dancing and seated Ganapatis were installed. These bore the names Ālayattu-Pillaiyār and Parivārālayattu-Pillaiyār.[2]

BIJA-GANAPATI OR VIJAYA-GANAPATI.

Ganapati, the Tamil Pillaiyār, is a very popular god. He is the god of wealth, the remover of all obstacles, the bestower of success, the fulfiller of desire. He is gentle, calm and friendly and withal possessed of a certain wise craft. A famous story relates how Vyāsa found no one capable of writing down his voluminous *Mahābhārata* to his dictation and was referred to Ganapati. Ganapati agreed, but on the understanding that Vyāsa never stopped for a moment in the midst. Vyāsa on his part stipulated that Ganapati should take down naught of which he did not understand the meaning. So whenever Vyāsa felt that he had to pause in the middle of his composition he gave out a more than ordinarily tough verse; and while the crafty god was worrying over its meaning managed to be ahead of the god's writing. Temples of Ganapati are quite common in Southern India, though there are none which may be considered particularly famous, except the one of Ucchi-Pillaiyār on the rock at Trichinopoly. In virtue of his being the lord of spirits *(ganas)* which cause obstacles to men, Ganapati is also considered to be the guardian deity of a village and is, as such, installed in one of the four quarters of almost every village.

---

[1] The Gānāpatyas recognize six forms of Ganapati to be the most important, viz., Mahā-Ganapati, Haridrā-Ganapati, Uchchhishta-Ganapati, Navanīta-Ganapati, Svarna-Ganapati and Santāna-Ganapati.

[2] I.e., Ganapati within the main temple and Ganapati in the surrounding shrines. Evidently the former was worshipped as a chief god and the latter as one of the subsidiary guardian deities of the temple.

XXVII

SKANDA OR KUMĀRA.

Skanda or Kumāra is another of Siva's sons known to Hindu mythology. He is represented with six faces (Shadānana) and as riding on a peacock. Being supposed to have been brought up by the six mothers, the *Krittikas* (Pleiades), he is known as Shānmātura and Kārttikēya. The *Purānas* state that he was born of the fiery energy of Siva in a forest of grass *(sara-vana)*, became the commander of the army of the gods in their battle against the giant Tāraka, and that he rent asunder by his arrows the mountain Krauncha. The birth of Skanda-Kumāra is described at great length by the famous poet Kālidāsa in his well-known work *Kumārasambhava*. Skanda is also known by the name Subrahmanya in the *Tantras*. In some unexplained way there exists an intimate connexion between the worship of Subrahmanya and of the serpent. The common name Subba or Subbarāya found among the Telugu, Canarese and Tamil people is explained to be both a contraction of Subrahmanya and a synonym for serpent. The sixth day of a lunar month *(shashthi)* is held as peculiarly sacred to Subrahmanya, as to the serpent god. His riding on a peacock, his marriage with the forest maid Valliyamman, and the fact that his most famous temples are on hill tops, show that he is connected with the ancient tree-and-serpent-worship and the sylvan deities. The *Silpasāra* describes him under name Subbarāya as having six faces, three eyes, the peacock vehicle and the weapons *sakti*, thunderbolt, sword, etc. The *Silpasangraha* describes him as having two arms, the sacred thread, a tuft, girdle, *kaupina* and staff like the unmarried students of the Vēdas *(brahmachārin)*. It may be noted that the day *shashthi*, sacred to serpent worship in Southern India, is celebrated by feeding *brahmachārins* and presenting cloths to them.

The *Kāsyapa-Silpa* sets down that the image of Skanda may be made of two, four, six or twelve hands and may have either six faces or only one. The symbols generally are the *sakti*, arrow, sword, discus, noose, a bunch of peacock's feathers, shield, bow, plough, rosary and the postures *abhaya* and *varada*. When the image has two hands, the left hand holds a cock *(kukkuta)* and the right hand a *sakti* (the Tamil *vēl)*[1]. Hēmādri speaks of him as wearing a red cloth and riding on a

[1] The famous image of Subrahmanya on the Palni Hills, called Palani-Āndavar, has only two arms in one of which he holds the *sakti*, the other resting freely on the waist.

peacock. The illustration from Tiruvottiyūr (fig. 113) shows only four hands.

SHADĀNANA-SUBRAHMANYA.

The most common variety however is the six-faced Shadānana-Subrahmanya, showing in his twelve hands the symbols and weapons, *sakti*, arrow, sword, discus, noose and *abhaya* on the right and a *kukktuta* (cock), bow, shield, conch, plough and *varada* on the left. He rides on the peacock vehicle and may have on either side of him the attendants Jaya and Vijaya (fig. 114), or perhaps the goddesses Vallī and Dēvayānā or Dēvasēnā, "the army of gods." A fine stone figure (fig. 115) of Kumāra on the peacock vehicle, with a single face and four arms and attended by the goddesses Vallī and Dēvayānā, comes from Samayapuram in the Trichinopoly district. A sketch from Chidambaram (fig. 116) shows Skanda with three visible faces, ten arms and the peacock vehicle fighting with giants—evidently Tāraka and his retinue. In four of his right hands he holds the weapons, sword, axe, arrow and club while the fifth is in the posture of pulling the bow string (missing in the illustration). The uppermost of his left arms shows the *vismaya* posture, and the four others hold the shield, bow, noose and bell. Subrahmanya may also be shown with one face and ten hands and riding on the peacock vehicle.

The worship of Skanda in India has been very ancient. Dr. Bhandarkar in his work *Vaishnavism*, *Saivism*, etc., has put forth literary and inscriptional evidence to prove that Skanda was worshipped in the time of Patanjali and in the early centuries of the Christian era. Sūdraka, the author of the drama *Mrichchhakatikā*, introducing a thief as one of the characters in his drama, makes him, before starting on his profession, invoke the blessings of Skanda. The artisans of the present day also resort to Skanda as one of the chief deities who preside over their craft. In the south the worship of Skanda-Kumāra under the name Vēlāyudha, Muruga, etc., is most popular. All classes are equally devoted to him, the non-Brahmans being particularly so. It may be noted that the shrines sacred to Skanda are always situated on hills, as at Tiruttani, Palnis, Tirupparangunram, Kunnakudi or on the seashore as at Tiruchchendūr, etc. An ancient Tamil poem called *Tirumurugārruppadai* probably written in the early eighth century A.D. is devoted exclusively to describing the shrines of Subrahmanya in Southern India. The god has been included in Aryan theogony from very early ages. Like most Saiva gods he may be the outcome of the fusion of the ancient Aryan and Dravidian cults and this may

FIG. 113.—Skanda ; Tiruvottiyūr.

FIG. 114.—Skanda (Shaḍānana): Madura.

FIG. 115.—Skanda and his consorts ; Samayapuram.

FIG. 116.—Skanda fighting with giants; Chidambaram.

account for the large number of devotees he claims among the non-Brahman classes of Southern India. Like the other Saiva attendants described above, who partake of the nature of Siva and are made of his substance, Skanda is also one of the leaders of the Saivite hosts *(ganas)*. He is a guardian deity and is enshrined in almost every Siva temple of importance in Southern India. He is *par excellence* the god of youth, of energy and virility.

CHAPTER V.

SAKTI-GODDESSES.

I

With each of the chief and minor gods described above are intimately connected one or more goddesses who, so far as the usual routine of worship in temples is concerned, play the subordinate part of consorts, but considered in the higher philosophical sense represent the peculiar energy or virtue of the god without which he could not be in active communion with the world. A cursory analysis of the Hindu cosmogony resolves itself into groups of gods and goddesses, the former being considered the agents or "the lords of *karma*" and the latter their inseparable power or source of energy. Thus Brahmā, the lord of creation, has the goddess Sarasvatī (the goddess of Learning or Speech) dwelling in his mouth. She presides over learning and is the *vāch, logos,* (word) which essentially is the first cause of creation ; so is Srī or Lakshmī, the consort of Vishnu, the presiding goddess of Wealth and Happiness and hence, also, the energy that sustains or keeps the world going. Siva's consort Pārvatī or Umā likewise, especially in her manifestation as Kālī, is the energy that destroys, that makes the world involve or draw itself into the quiescent state from which it started or evolved. In fact a sect of worshippers called Sāktas, "the adherents of Sakti or Energy," affirm that this Sakti, the feminine element in god, is the sole, if not the preponderating, cause of all visible phenomena. It may be noted that the word *sakti* is of the feminine gender in the Sanskrit language. Almost every human or divine activity has been personified as a goddess ; even the letters of the alphabet being supposed to have their presiding deities. This theory of goddesses has pervaded even Jainism and Buddhism, the latter especially in its Mahāyāna development. Strict Sakti-worshippers do not make any distinction of caste and creed. Perhaps it was thus that Sakti-faith became one of the compromises providing a common meeting ground for the different forms of religion prevailing in India.[1]

---

1 *Mayūrabhanja*, Introduction, p. lxii.

Germs of the energy-creed may indeed be traced even in the Upanishads—the early sacred books of the Hindus—though its extreme development took place at a much later period.

II

Saktis may be found depicted in temples in any one of the three aspects, the calm, the terrible or the ugly, as distinguished by the particular positions in which they are placed or the circumstances under which they are worshipped. When merely represented as the consorts of the gods they are mild and pleasing in appearance and have only two hands, in one of which is held the lotus bud. More often, however, the goddesses have independent existence. The majority of these latter are Saivite in their nature, i.e., wild, fearful and destructive and are often propitiated only by bloody sacrifices.[1] Before entering upon a description of these numerous Saivite Saktis, a word may be said of each of the milder ones associated with Brahmā, Vishnu and Siva. It must be noted that the characteristic feature in the worship of Saktis, whether Saivite, Vaishnavite or otherwise, is the association with them of mystic charms, or geometrical figures called *chakras, yantras* or *pithas*, with conventional and often mystic incantations and solemn ceremonials which make no appeal to the gentler feelings of human nature.

III

SARASVATI or VĀGISVARI.

Sarasvatī or Vāgīsvarī, the consort of Brahmā, may be represented with two or more hands. In the former case she holds the book and the rosary, and in the latter the noose and the hook in addition (fig. 117).[2] Vāgīsvarī, who is referred to in *Mayūrabhanja* (Introduction, p. lxxvi) as a goddess worshipped both by the Buddhist and Hindu *Tāntrikas*, is described in the *Pāncharātrāgama* as having three eyes and four hands holding in these latter the staff, book, rosary and the water-pot, which as we have seen above, are the symbols of the creator Brahmā. Two other allied forms of Vāgīsvarī are Dhēnu-Vāgīsvarī and Saubhāgya-Vāgīsvarī, both of which are mild in appearance and beautiful, but as Saktis in essence, they display the Saivaite attributes of three eyes, the *jatāmakuta*

---

1 A recognized classification of the Saktis under the heads Yōga, Bhōga and Vīra has been already referred to (above, p. 110, note 2). The first is defined to be the goddess who is identical with the pedestal of Siva; the second is the goddess that stands to the left of Siva or the Siva-*linga* as his consort and the third is the independent goddess generally installed in the third outer *prākāra* of Siva temples.

2 In certain cases where she is represented with four hands, she holds the *vīnā* and the water-pot.

FIG. 117.—Sarasvatī ; Bāgali.

and the crescent. The former, who is *logos* (Sabda-Brahmā) incarnate, is identical with the illustration from Bāgali given above. Sarasvatī, when represented as the goddess Sārada (the form in which she is worshipped at Sringēri-matha, in Mysore) presiding over the sixty-four sciences (*chatushshashtikalā*), has five faces and ten arms. The worship of Sarasvatī generally held on the ninth day of the Dasara is conducted by invoking her presence in a library of books and offering fruits, flowers, sandal and incense.

IV

LAKSHMĪ OR SRĪ AND PRITHVĪ OR MAHĪ.

The two consorts of Vishnu are Lakshmī (Wealth) and Prithvī (Earth). The former is seated or standing on a red lotus pedestal, has four hands, holds two lotus flowers in her upper arms, the other two hands being either in the boon-giving and protecting postures or holding a vessel and a fruit. She is said to have sprung from the ocean at the time of its being churned for nectar. The latter, Prithvī,[1] has only two hands of which the right is raised in the *abhaya* posture and the left holds the fruit of the pomegranate. Her left leg is represented also as stepping upon a pot of treasures. When Lakshmī accompanies Vishnu she has only two hands. Eight forms of Lakshmī, known as Ashta-Mahālakshmī, are recognized. Of these, Gaja-Lakshmī is the most popular. She is generally found figured on the lintels of door-frames, has four arms and is seated in the same posture as Vināyaka, on a full-blown lotus of eight petals. In her right hand she holds a lotus flower with a long stem which reaches her shoulder ring and in her left a pot of nectar. The two other hands of the goddess hold the *bilva*-fruit and the conch. Behind her are represented two elephants pouring water from two pots held by their trunks over the head of the goddess. The *Mānasāra* describes the same goddess with two hands as Sāmānya-Lakshmī and says that she is figured on door-ways. In the *Silpasāra* this goddess is called the two-handed Indra-Lakshmī. A fine representation of Sāmānya-Lakshmī comes from Mahābalipuram (fig. 118).[2] The central figure of the group is seated on a pedestal of lotus flower, whose open petals are seen hanging down and decorating with their edges the rim of another lotus pedestal at the

GAJA-LAKSHMĪ.

SĀMĀNYA-LAKSHMĪ; INDRA-LAKSHMĪ.

---

[1] *Mānasāra* describing her under the name Mahī says, that she is figured standing or seated to the left of Vishnu with a blue lotus in her right hand, the left hand hanging down or showing the *varada* posture.

[2] *Mayūrabhanja*, Introduction, p. lxvi.

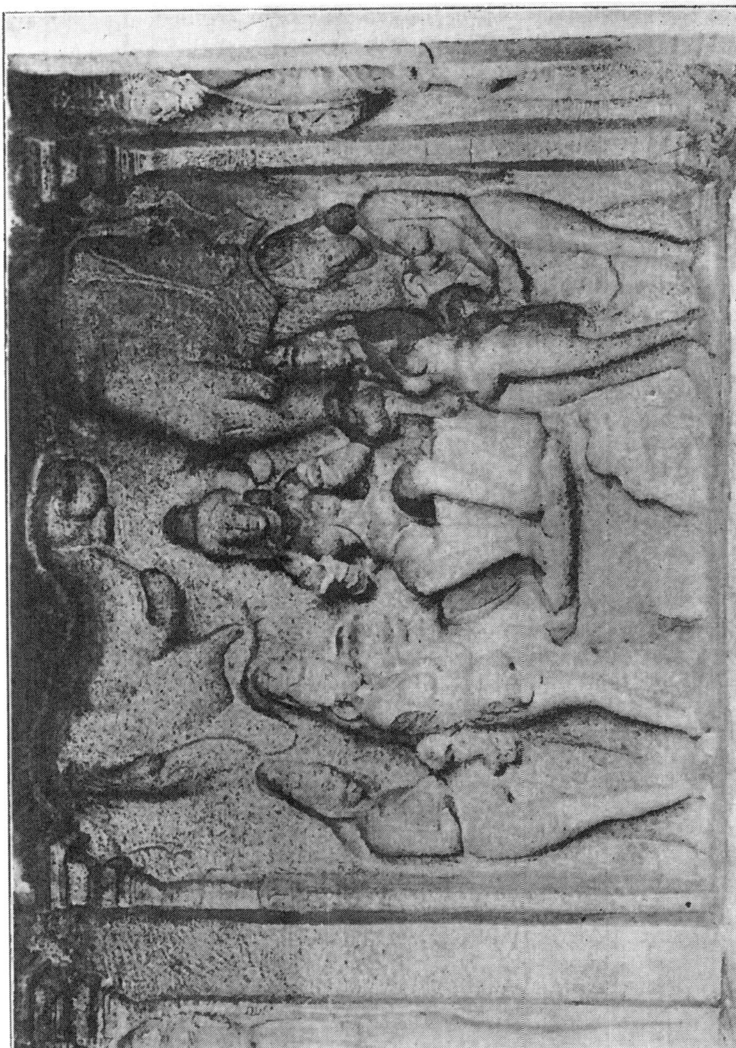

FIG. 118.—Sāmānya-Lakshmī; Seven Pagodas.

base. Below this again is a floral design, also perhaps of lotuses, a bud in the middle and full blown flowers on either side. The goddess has two hands and holds in each of them a closed lotus flower. Two female attendants on the immediate right and left sides are seen lifting up pots of water which are received by two majestic elephants in their trunks (not fully represented) and poured over the head of the goddess alternately. The second female attendant to the left of the goddess carries a lotus bud in one of her hands, and the corresponding one to the right, a cup-like vessel, which in all probability is meant to hold the sandal paste, turmeric powder or some toilet requisite intended for the goddess. The head dress of the attendant women and the simple ornaments which they wear are worth noting and point to the modest taste of the Pallava times. The *Sri-sūkta* praises Lakshmī as "the goddess of Prosperity standing on the lotus flower, slightly bent on account of the weight of her breasts, having high hips, broad lotus-like eyes and deep navel pit, dressed in white cloth and bathed by heavenly elephants from golden pots which are bedecked with a variety of jewels, and holding lotuses in her hands." Havell calls the picture from Mahābalipuram "Lakshmī arising from the sea" and describes it in Chapter XXI of his *Ideals of Indian Art*. Another of the eight Lakshmīs, is Mahā-Lakshmī who has four hands in which she holds a vessel, the club *Kaumōdaki*, the shield and the *bēl*-fruit *(srīphala)*. A special feature of this Mahā-Lakshmī is that she wears a *linga* on her head. When standing or seated on a lotus, with lotus flowers in her two upper hands and the *varada* and *abhaya* postures in the lower, Lakshmī receives the name Vīra-Lakshmī. In another representation she holds the noose, rosary, lotus and the hook. Kollāpura-Mahālakshmī is stated in the *Silpasāra* to have six arms, in three of which are held the club, shield and wine-cup. Another called Ashtabhujā-Vīralakshmī has eight arms, in which are seen the noose, hook, rosary, the boon-conferring hand, the hand of protection, the club, lotus and the vessel.

Mahā-Lakshmī. **Vīra-Lakshmī.** **Kollāpura-Mahā-Lakshmī.**

The eight Energies of Vishnu.

The Padma-*Purāna* mentions eight Saktis (or Energies) of the protecting god Vishnu, viz., Srī, Bhū, Sarasvatī, Prīti, Kīrti, Sānti, Tushti and Pushti. As the names clearly indicate, these goddesses of Wealth, Earth, Learning, Love, Fame, Peace, Pleasure and Strength are the eight channels through which the protective energies of Vishnu are brought into play. All these goddesses have four hands, hold lotuses in the two upper ones and exhibit the *varada* and *abhaya* postures in the two lower.

V

GAURĪ OR PĀRVATĪ.

The general form of the goddess Gaurī, Pārvatī or Umā, the consort of Siva, as given in the *Kāsyapa-Silpa* and the *Mānasāra*, is that she has two hands when accompanying the god Siva and four when represented independently. In the former case she is fully decorated, is standing or seated on a lotus pedestal, holds a blue lily in the right hand, while her left hangs down loose "like the tail of a cow." She wears a band on the forehead called *phālapatta*, has one of her legs slightly bent *(kunchita)* and the other placed straight *(lambita* or *svastika)* on the pedestal; she stands to the left of the image of Siva or the Siva-*linga* and wears the head-dress *karandamakuta, kirītamakuta* or *kēsabandha* (fig. 119). In the latter case also she is fully decorated, has a *jatāmakuta* like a male deity, and presents with her lower hands the *varada* and *abhaya* postures, while in the upper two she holds the red and the blue lotuses. Earlier authorities state that she may also exhibit in these hands the lily and the rosary. The illustration from Paramēsvaramangalam (fig. 120) shows in the upper hands the noose and the hook. Gaurī is usually represented with the ornaments of an unmarried girl (*kanyakā*), sometimes doing penance with the object of securing Siva for her husband (fig. 121), and in this form she is worshipped by the Māhēsvaras.

VI

The Saivite goddesses, who are either the independent manifestations of Pārvatī or the dependent groups of her following, are too many to mention.[1] Most of the village goddesses mentioned in Chapter VI, below, will be counted by the orthodox Brāhmana among these classes.

The SAPTAMĀTRIKAS, "Seven Mothers."

We may begin the description of the Saivite Sakti deities with the group of goddesses known as Saptamātrikās,[2] or the "Seven Mothers." They are:—Brāhmī, Māhēsvarī, Kaumārī Vaishnavī, Vārāhī, Māhēndrī and Chāmundā.[3] These with Mahā-Lakshmī, described below, are sometimes counted as "Eight Mothers." They have generally two hands, are red in

[1] Hēmādri, for instance, has included names such as Vāmā, Jyēshthā, Raudrī, Kālī, Kalavikaranī, Balavikaranī, Balapramathanī, Sarvabhūtadamanī and Manōnmanī which are merely different synonyms of Siva, with the feminine terminations added on to them.

[2] See Burgess's *Elura Cave Temples*, Plate XXXIV.

[3] Nārasimhī with the face of the man-lion god Narasimha is sometimes mentioned in place of Chāmundā. It is also sometimes stated that the Seven Mothers are but different forms of Chandī (i.e. Chāmundā).

FIG. 119.—Pārvatī ; Bōlumāmpatti.

FIG. 120.—Pārvatī; Paramēśvaramangalam.

FIG. 121.—Pârvatî in penance; Pattisvaram.

colour and hold a skull and a lotus. Some authorities like the *Silpasangraha* state that as representing the active energy of Brahmā, Mahēsvara, Kumāra, Vishnu, etc., they have the same vehicles as their lords and hold the same weapons. Brāhmī (also called Brahmānī) consequently has four faces, six arms[1] and the swan vehicle, and she is of yellow hue. Māhēsvarī (Bhairavī) rides on a bull, has five faces, three eyes and ten arms, and is decorated with the crescent. Kaumārī has six faces and twelve arms and rides on a peacock. Vaishnavī is of blue colour and rides on Garuda, has six arms and the garland of flowers called *vanamālā* (peculiar to Vishnu). Vārāhī has the face of a sow,[2] is black in colour, has a big protruding belly and rides on a buffalo.[3] Māhēndrī (Indrānī) has a thousand eyes, like her consort Indra, is of pleasing appearance and of golden hue, and rides on an elephant. She has apparently also six arms and displays the symbols *varada*, noose and thunderbolt in her right arms and the *abhaya*, vessel and lotus in her left. Chāmundā[4] is black and fearful with protruding teeth, long tongue, erect hair, emaciated body, sunken red eyes and a withered belly. It is stated that she can change her appearance at will. She rides on a corpse, wears a garland of skulls and has jewels of serpents. In her ten arms she holds the shield, noose, bow, staff and spear on the left side, and the pestle, disc, fly-whisk, goad and sword on the right. The *Mayamata* adds that she wears a tiger's skin, has red hair glowing like fire, and the banner of a kite. She may have four, eight or ten hands. According to the same authority these Seven Mothers are to be flanked by Vīrabhadra and Vināyaka on either side (fig. 122). In front of the Saptamātrikās the god Siva may be seated on a lotus flower under the banyan tree. Some of these goddesses are

---

[1] The illustration in the *Elura Cave Temples* shows only four hands.

[2] In the panel of Saptamātrikās (*ibid.* Plate XXXIV, No. 1) Vārāhī is represented with a fine human face and the usual ornaments but has the sow-vehicle. In No. 3 on the same plate, however, the goddess has the face of a sow.

[3] The *Silpasangraha* says that Vārāhī was born of Yāma, the God of Death. According to Hēmādri the goddess Yāmyā, evidently identical with Vārāhī, rides on the buffalo, holds a staff and drinks blood from a skull. Three other goddesses with sow-face are mentioned in the *Lalitōpākhyāna* and the *Vārāhikalpa*. Dandanātha-Vārāhī is one, seated on the golden lotus. She has eight arms and a staff by her side. Svapna-Vārāhī has the gleaming tusks of a sow and four arms. She rides on a horse. Suddha-Vārāhī has also tusks and four arms. It may be noted that Bārtālī (Battālī) is a Buddhist goddess of similar description, sometimes also referred to in the Hindu *Tantras* (*Mayūrabhanja*, Introduction, p. xcv).

[4] This image has perhaps to be distinguished from Mahishāsuramardinī-Chāmundā described below.

FIG. 122.—The Seven Mothers; Tanjore.

said to have each a tree specially sacred to them, e.g., Kaumārī has the fig-tree *(udumbara)*, Vaishnavī, the *pipal*, Vārāhī, the *karanja*, Indrānī, the celestial tree *kalpadruma*, and Chāmundā, the banyan.

The Saptamātrikās thus described are generally found figured together in a group on the same panel and are quite a common sight in South-Indian villages and Siva temples. When installed within the enclosure of a temple, they are seen often without a shrine built over them, and may receive such attention as the other minor deities of that temple. In villages and in Pidāri temples built exclusively for goddesses, they are worshipped regularly. The Selliyamma temple at Ālambākkam in the Tanjore district possesses an important shrine for the Saptamātrikās. The order in which the Saptamātrikā images are cut on the stone differs according to circumstances. For the destruction of enemies and safety to villages Brāhmī or Brahmānī must be made to occupy the centre. If Chāmundā be placed there instead, the village will grow in population.

At the entrances to the shrines of Saptamātrikās are placed two guardian deities. Evil spirits, demons and demi-gods, holding tridents in their hands, may also be installed in the same place. It is enjoined that the daily worship and festivities in the Saptamātrikā shrines are to be performed according to rules prescribed by the *Yāmala-mantrasāstra*.

VII

Sakti-goddesses with Vaishnavite symbols.

The following three goddesses, viz., Durgā, Chāmundā and Mahishāsuramardinī, though they partake mainly of the nature of Pārvatī,[1] are however seen holding the Vaishnavite symbols of the discus and the conch. The *Purānas* say that Durgā was born of Yasōdā, in order to save the life of Krishna who was just then born to Dēvakī. The children were exchanged under divine intervention. Kamsa, the cruel brother of Dēvakī, who had vowed to kill all the children of his sister, thought this female child was Dēvakī's and dashed it against a stone; but, then, the child flew into the air and assuming the form of Durgā mocked him and went away. On account of this incident she is known as the sister of Vāsudēva-Krishna. The *Silpasāra* mentions a Chandikā (Chāmundā) of eighteen arms to whom the god Siva presented the trident, Krishna (Vishnu), the conch and Agni,

[1] It is stated that the active energy of Siva, which is Vishnu himself, receives the name Kālī while it assumes an angry mood, that in battles it is recognized as Durgā and that in peace and pleasure it takes the form Bhavānī (i.e. Pārvatī).

the weapon called *sakti*. According to the Mārkandēya-*Purāna* the goddess that killed the buffalo-demon (Mahishāsuramardinī) was made up of the fierce radiance of Siva, Vishnu and Brahmā while all the other gods contributed the powers peculiarly characteristic of them for the formation of her limbs and ornaments.

CHĀMUNDĀ. Chāmundā[1] may be represented with eight, ten (fig. 123), twelve or sixteen arms and made either of wood or of mortar. When in the dancing posture she must have eight, six or four hands. Chāmundā is known by the name Karālī or Bhadrakālī when she has eight arms, Kālabhadrā when she has six arms, and Kālī, when she has four. BHADRAKĀLĪ. Bhadrakālī has a terrible face, fat breasts, protruding teeth and a long tongue and wears a garland of skulls. She rides on a lion and stamps under her foot the head of the buffalo-demon. Hēmādri quoting the *Vishnudharmōttara* says that Bhadrakālī has eighteen arms and is seated in the *ālidha* posture in a car drawn by four lions. When worshipped by Brāhmanas she has ten arms, the *jatāmakuta* and all ornaments. KĀLABHADRĀ. The second, Kālabhadrā, has a beautiful white form but is fierce, being worshipped in burial-grounds under the name of Karālabhadrā, seated in the *virāsana* posture with the foot placed over the head of the buffalo-demon. The same goddess, when worshipped by the Kshatriyas, is called Kālī or Mahākālī.[2] KĀLĪ OR MAHĀKĀLĪ. In this form she ordinarily holds a trident or sword in one hand and a skull or a cup of wine (fire ?) in the other, rides on a corpse and has a lean stomach. The owl is her vehicle. She wears the tiger's skin, a scarf of elephant's hide and a garland of heads; has three eyes and ear-ornaments shaped like conches; and is fond of flesh, blood and life. She is followed by evil spirits who fill the four quarters with their roar and she roams about the earth riding on their shoulders. Hēmādri, calling her also by the name Sivarātrī, describes her as having four hands, being black like collyrium, terrible with protruding teeth and tongue (but at the same time beautiful with broad eyes and slender waist), wearing a garland of trunks (of human bodies) and a wreath of serpents.

---

[1] Chāmundā is supposed to be the form of Pārvatī when she killed the giant called Chanda-Munda.

[2] Mahākālī is described in the *Chandīkalpa* as having ten faces, ten legs and ten arms in which are held all weapons of war. In this form she is stated to have been invoked by Brahmā to kill the demons Madhu and Kaitabha who were attempting to smash Vishnu in his sleep (see above, p. 52). The *Kāranāgama* mentions an eight-armed Kālī or Mahākālī among the Durgās. Kālikā is a goddess supposed to be the wife of Nairrita (below, p. 243).

FIG. 123.—Chāmuṇḍā (Mahākāli); Tiruchchengōḍu.

Kālī represented sometimes also with twelve or sixteen arms is worshipped by the Vaisyas and Sūdras under the names Charcharā and Bhairavī respectively.

Durgā is a very popular deity. The name is indifferently applied to all goddesses with a terrible appearance and in a fighting attitude. The general description of Durgā given in the *Kāsyapa-Silpa* represents her as having four arms, two eyes, high hips, high breasts, and all ornaments. She holds the conch and the discus in her upper hands,[1] while her right lower hand presents the *abhaya* posture and the left lower rests on the waist. She stands on a lotus-pedestal and has a breast-band of serpents and a red petticoat. According to the *Silparatna*, Mūla-Durgā holds in her lower hands the bow and the arrow. From Mahābalipuram comes the figure of a Durgā (fig. 124) who stands on the buffalo's head. She has eight arms, in the uppermost of which are found the discus and the conch. The other weapons held are the sword and the bell on the right side and the bow and shield on the left. The lowest of the right hands holds evidently a *sriphala* or the *bēl*-fruit and the corresponding left has a parrot perching on it and rests freely on the waist of the goddess. The necklace, breast-band and the garment hanging in folds down to her feet deserve to be noticed. The absence of finger rings on the eight hands of the goddess is peculiar. The illustration shows also other figures surrounding the goddess, viz., two male devotees with peculiar head dress kneeling at her feet, two female attendants on either side holding the sword and the bow, two demi-gods one of whom is carrying a *chauri*, and a lion and a deer. In another *mandapa* at Mahābalipuram is a sculpture evidently of the same goddess with the lion and the deer, pairs of demi-gods on the sides and devotees at the feet, one of whom is in the act of either cutting off his hair or his neck. The goddess has only four arms and stands on an ordinary pedestal but not on the buffalo's head (fig. 125). At Srīmushnam in the South Arcot district is an image of Durgā with eight arms showing almost the same symbols as those of the figure at Mahābalipuram described above, the only exception being that instead of the bell in one of the right

DURGĀ.

MŪLA-DURGĀ.

[1] Rai Bahadur Venkayya says in *South-Ind. Inscrs.*, Vol. II. Introd., p. 41, note 1:—"Durgā is represented with a sheep's head standing on the giant Simhamukhāsura whom she killed. Her head is fiery and adorned with different jewels. On her forehead she wears a crescent made with sacred ashes of burnt cow-dung. In five of her six hands she holds, respectively, a ring, a sword, a trident, a goad, and a skull."

FIG. 124.—Durgā; Seven Pagodas.

FIG. 125. - Durgā ; Seven Pagodas.

hands she is holding, perhaps more correctly, the arrow. The figure stands on the head of a buffalo without any other accompanying attendants and has an umbrella overhead (fig. 126). Images of Durgā with four or more arms standing on the head of a buffalo are generally found placed in a niche on the north wall of the central shrine of Siva temples in Southern India (fig. 127). Occasionally, however, they may stand on ordinary pedestals without the buffalo's head, as at Tiruvottiyūr near Madras. In the Vishnu temple at Tirumalisai, Chingleput district, is a similar image (fig. 128) placed in a niche on the north wall of the central shrine. It is said to be Lakshmī but perhaps represents Durgā without the

KĀTYĀYANĪ. buffalo's head. The *Mayamata*, describing the figure of Kātyāyanī with four arms, says that she holds the conch and the discus in the upper hands and exhibits the *abhaya* and the *varada* postures with the lower. With eight arms and a parrot, this same figure is stated to receive the name of Durgā. The description of the sculptures from Mahābalipuram and Srīmushnam agrees with what has been said of Kātyāyanī in the *Mayamata*.

The *Saivāgama* specifically describes nine varieties of Durgā, all of which have two arms but different weapons

SAILAPUTRĪ. and vehicles. The first, known as Sailaputrī, rides on a bull, wears the crescent on her head and holds a trident in her hand; the second Brahmachārinī holds the rosary and the water-pot; the third Chandakhandā rides on the kite and has an angry look; the fourth Skandamātā rides on a lion and holds lotus buds in her hands; the fifth Kūshmānda-Durgā is distinguished by a pot full of wine (or blood) which she holds in both of her hands; the sixth Kātyāyanī riding on a tiger, holds a drawn sword in her hands and is killing a giant; the seventh Kālarātrī is of fearful appearance and has a grim smile on her face; the eighth Mahā-Gaurī rides on a white elephant; and the ninth Siddhidāyinī is attended by demi-gods. The *Kāranāgama* quoting the *Skanda-Yāmala* describes these nine Durgās under different names and says that one of them has eighteen arms while the rest have sixteen each. They are generally shown standing naked with one leg placed on the head of the buffalo-demon and hold in their fist a tuft of the giant's hair. One of the Durgās with sixteen arms called Shōdasabhujā-Durgā has three eyes and serpent-jewellery and holds tridents in all her sixteen arms.

MAHISHĀSURAMARDINĪ. Mahishāsuramardinī (also called Chāmundā, Chandī) is represented in the *Nrisimhaprāsāda* as the youthful but angry form of Pārvatī with three broad eyes, a slender waist, heaving breasts, one face and twenty hands. Below her is the

FIG. 126.—Durgā ; Srimushnam.

FIG. 127.—Durgâ ; Dhârâsuram.

FIG. 128.—Durga-Lakshmi; Tirumalisai.

buffalo-demon with his head cut off and rolling on the ground. A man emerging from the buffalo's neck is seen holding a weapon in his hand, abject with fear. Pierced by the trident of the goddess, he is vomiting blood. The lion too on which Chandikā is riding attacks the giant with its mouth while the noose held by the goddess is tightly fastened round his neck. The goddess's right leg is placed on the lion while the other steps on the body of the demon.[1] This form of Chandī is propitiated by those who wish to destroy their enemies. The ruling family of Mysore has Chāmundā-Chandī for its tutelary deity.

MAHĀ-LAKSHMĪ.

A goddess with sixteen arms killing the buffalo-demon and as such to be classed among the Saivite Saktis, is also called Mahā-Lakshmī. The Mahā-Lakshmī, described in the *Chandikalpa*, has twenty arms, holds all the destructive weapons and is seen in the act of killing the buffalo-demon.[2] It will be observed that this Mahā-Lakshmī is only another form of Durgā.

Various postures of Mahishāsuramardinī in the act of killing the buffalo-demon are depicted in South-Indian Saiva temples, some of them being of excellent workmanship. It is not always easy to distinguish the images which are thus engaged in the act of killing the buffalo-demon, and to say whether they be representations of Chāmundā, Durgā, Mahishāsuramardinī or Mahā-Lakshmī. It may, however, be suggested that figures with a breast-band standing upright on the severed head of the buffalo are generally those of Durgā-Lakshmī, while those in the actual fighting attitude are either Chāmundā, Mahishāsuramardinī or Mahā-Lakshmī. They generally have eight arms and hold weapons, the conch, discus, bow, shield, sword, bell, noose and trident. The demon may be shown with a human body, or a human body with a buffalo's head,[3] or a buffalo from whose severed trunk proceeds a human figure. The illustrations given show some of the fighting postures of Mahishāsuramardinī (figs. 129, 130, 131). In the Mahishāsura-*mandapa* at Mahābalipuram is seen a relief on the proper left wall, which represents the fight between Durgā-Mahishāsuramardinī and the

---

[1] Hēmādri speaking of Kātyāyanī with ten arms, gives almost the same description.

[2] Mahā-Sarasvatī mentioned in the same work, is said to be an emanation of Gaurī. She has eight arms and is engaged in destroying the demon Sumbha and his retinue.

[3] Burgess's *Elura Cave Temples*, Plate IV, fig. 7, shows the giant as a man with buffalo's horns.

FIG. 129.—Mahishâsuramardinî ; Gangaikondasōlapuram.

FIG. 130.—Mahishâsuramardinî ; Dhârâsuram.

FIG. 131.—Mahishâsuramardini ; Durgi.

FIG. 132.—Durgā-Mahishāsuramardini ; Seven Pagodas.

buffalo-demon (fig. 132). Dr. Vogel gives the following description of the relief:—"The goddess astride on her vehicle, the lion, is eight-armed. With two hands she shoots arrows at the demon king. The emblems held in her remaining six arms are a disc (*chakra*), a bell (*ghantā*) and a sword (*khadga*) to the right and a conch (*sankha*), a noose (*pāsa*) and an indistinct object, to the left. A quiver is visible over her left shoulder.

"She is surrounded by a host of dwarfs, evidently the *ganas* of Siva, her spouse. One, behind her, holds a parasol over her head, another at her side waves a fly-whisk (*chāmara*). The remainder carry weapons, usually a round buckler and a curved sword, in shape like the *kukri* of the Gurkhas. One in the foreground is in the act of shooting an arrow from a bow.

"Distinct from these *ganas* is a female figure fallen on her knees in front of the lion and raising a sword with her right hand. Possibly this figure represents Kālī, an emanation of Durgā, though she does not present the terrific appearance peculiar to the black goddess.

"Right opposite Durgā stands the colossal figure of the buffalo-headed demon-king. His royal rank also is indicated by a parasol held over his head. He carries a heavy mace in his two hands and has, moreover, a sword fastened to his left hip. His attitude is that of yielding to the onslaught of the warlike goddess.

"His army is represented by seven demons. Two of these are prostrated in the foreground—one slain and another wounded. The latter raises his right hand with two fingers raised. What is the meaning of this gesture? Is it that of a vanquished warrior imploring his victorious enemy to spare his life? Of the remaining *asuras* one is retreating, whereas the others seem to offer a feeble resistance. It is worthy of notice that with the exception of Mahishāsura himself, the demons are shown in a purely human shape."

VIII

Many other Saivite goddesses of fearful appearance, worshipped by people who wish to destroy their enemies or to receive some desired object of life, are described in the *Tāntrik* works. Some of these which are mentioned below may possibly be, as some suggest, the Aryanized forms of aboriginal deities still worshipped in the Pidāri temples of the South.

Kālarātrī already referred to as one of the nine Durgās, has a single braid of hair and *japā*-flowers for her ear-ornaments; she is naked, rides on an ass, has hanging lips KĀLARĀTRĪ.

and is bathed in oil. In her left hand she holds a human head severed from the body and on the left leg is worn an anklet of metallic wire.

TVARITĀ. Tvaritā is stated to be a goddess of the Kirātas or a 'hunters.' She has two hands, is decorated with peacock's feathers on the head, and wears a cloth of leaves (as some of the wild tribes of to-day), a garland of *gunjā*-seeds and a (head) jewel of eight serpents. Nagendra Natha Vasu finds in this goddess a close resemblance to Nāgamātā "the mother of serpents," Skandashashthi or Manasā, and to the goddess Tavitā of the Scythians.[1]

TRIPURĀ-BHAIRAVĪ. Tripurā-Bhairavī has four arms, wears a garland of heads and has her breasts bathed in blood.

VAJRAPRASTĀRINĪ. Vajraprastārinī[2] is stated to be seated on a lotus, in a boat of blood floating in an ocean of blood. The limbs of her body as well as her head are also bathed in blood.

SURĀ. Surā, wine personified, is represented as a terrible unmarried goddess of eighteen arms and of three eyes. She is tall of form and is as dangerous as destructive fire. She is a terror to the demons and a blessing to angels. In plain language Umā herself is described to be the goddess of wine and Siva (her consort) to be the power of intoxication thereof.

SURAPRIYĀ. Surapriyā is a goddess seated in a meditative posture cross-legged and attended by a group of Saktis called Ashtāngayoginīs. On either side of her are the deities Pūrnāsvā and Pushkalā. Madhukara, a fat man with hanging belly, two hands and a smiling face, stands on the left side of the goddess. A pot of wine and a staff are also placed near her. The goddess is installed in the houses of prostitutes and small villages or towns, under different names such as Dēvabhāvi, Jnānabhāvi and Gītabhāvi.[3]

SRĪVIDYĀ-DĒVĪ. Srīvidyādēvī has fierce fangs protruding from her mouth, sits on a serpent couch and wears necklaces of human bones.

PRĀNASAKTI. Prānasakti, like Vajraprastārinī, is seated on a lotus springing from a boat of blood, in an ocean of blood, and holds among other weapons a human skull filled with blood.

---

[1] *Mayūrabhanja*, Introduction, p. xxxix f. The *Silparatna* adds that Tvaritā rides on a crow and is considered to be a widow.

[2] According to the *Silparatna* this goddess is a form of Pārvatī, has six hands, is seated on a red lotus, exhibits in her hands a sugarcane-bow, a flower-arrow, the *varada* and *abhaya* postures, a noose and a skull, and is engaged in vanquishing Māra—the god of Love.

[3] In the names Pūrnāsvā, Pushkalā and Madhukara we may see an apparent analogy to Pūranai, Pudgalai and Madurai-Vīran mentioned under village deities (below, p. 230).

This is, as it should be, in the case of a goddess who presides over the centres of physical life *(prāna)*.[1]

Svasthāvēsinī is of scarlet colour, inspires dread in those who see her, dwells amidst corpses, has three faces and two arms holding the kettle-drum and the trident, dark eyes, lean body and three braids of thick black hair. She is of the nature of forest fire. SVASTHA-VĒSINĪ.

Satruvidhvamsinī, "the destroyer of enemies," has likewise three faces, is as cruel as the flames of fire, has red eyes, fearful fangs, red hair, and a capacious belly. She is naked. SATRUVIDH-VAMSINĪ.

Ugra-Tārā, the goddess presiding over various diseases, stands in the *ālīdha* posture, carries a corpse over her head and roars terribly. Short of stature, she has braids of black colour mixed with yellow and is surrounded by dreadful serpents. In a skull she holds the diseases of the three worlds together, with the object of killing them. UGRA-TĀRĀ

Dhūmrāvatī or Dhūmra-Kālī has a red body and wears a red cloth. Her ear-rings are like the trunks of an elephant and her fangs, terrible. She wears a necklace of skulls, is surrounded by devils, and holds in her hands a drawn sword and a skull. DHŪMRA-VATĪ.

Sūlinī with her eight arms, is likewise a goddess who inspires fear. She holds a trident, rides on a lion and is accompanied by four unmarried girls with swords and shields in their hands. SŪLINĪ.

Pratyangirā has four arms and a face as terrible as that of a lion. Her hair stands erect on her head. In her hands she holds a skull, trident, kettle-drum and the noose *(nāgapāsa)*. She is seated on a lion and by her power destroys all enemies (figs. 133 and 134).[2] PRATYAN-GIRĀ.

Sītalādēvī (or Māriyamma), the goddess of small-pox, is represented as riding naked on an ass with a winnow on her head and a broom and water-pot in her hands.[3] SĪTALĀDĒVĪ.

Trikantakīdēvī has a body which is black below the navel, red between the navel and the neck and white above it. The terrible fangs protruding from her four faces are so long and crooked that they pierce out through her belly. In her four hands she holds two lamps, a conch and a discus. TRIKANTAKĪ-DĒVĪ.

---

[1] The goddess Prānasakti is invoked by Brāhmanas, in ceremonies where the *prānapratishthā*, "infusing (an image) with life," has to be observed.

[2] The lion vehicle is missing in the Tiruppalātturai bronze. The Tiruchchengōdu figure has the sword and shield in place of skull and noose and a breast-band like Durgā. Both are called Bhadrakālī by the people.

[3] The illustration of this image given by Nagendra Natha Vasu (*Mayūrabhanja*, Plate, facing p. xcvi, fig. 51) and classed by him as one of the Buddhist and *Tāntrik* goddesses, is not naked. Neither does she carry a winnow on her head.

FIG. 133.--Pratyangirā; Tiruchchengōdu

FIG. 134.—Pratyangirā (?) (metal); Tiruppalāttuṛai.

BHŪTAMĀTĀ. Bhūtamātā, "the mother of goblins" has her seat under a *pipal*-tree and is followed by numerous demons, goblins and demi-gods. She has two hands in which are held a *linga* (or, sometimes a sword) and the shield. She rides on the lion and has dishevelled hair.

SIVADŪTĪ. Sivadūtī has a dejected appearance, emaciated body and the face of a jackal. She wears a garland of skulls, is fearful and is surrounded by serpents. She may have four or more arms,[1] holding in the former case, a vessel of blood, the sword, the trident and a flesh-pot.

IX

JYĒSHTHĀ OR JYĒSHTHĀ-LAKSHMĪ. Jyēshthā or Jyēshthā-Lakshmī, so called on account of her being supposed to be the elder sister of Lakshmī,[2] is a black goddess with hanging lips, stunted nose, pendant breasts and a big belly. She revels in blood. In one hand she holds a lotus made of iron while the other hand rests on her seat. But sometimes she is seen holding lotuses in both her hands. The legs of the goddess are stretched and hang down from the seat, in the so-called European fashion. Her parting curly hair is made up in the form *vāsikābandha*. A pair of crows represents her banner. On her right side is seated a bull-faced figure said to be her son, holding a staff in the right hand and exhibiting a pointing finger *(sūchi)* in the left. On the corresponding left side of Jyēshthā, is seated her daughter, said to be a fair lady (fig. 135). Sometimes the goddess is represented as red in colour and then receives the name Rakta-Jyēshthā. The goddess Jyēshthā with the hanging belly, attended by women on either side and wearing a red cloth, is generally installed outside villages. Her following consists of goblins, demons and spirits. She is the goddess of ill-luck.[3]

The worship of Jyēshthā appears to have been once quite familiar in the Tamil country. Like the shrines of Pidāri, her shrines were also exempted from taxation, as stated in early Chōla records. From an inscription on a pillar in the rock-cut temple of Subrahmanyasvāmin at Tirupparangunram near Madura, we learn that about the eighth century A.D. a shrine

---

[1] A Sivadūtī of eight arms is mentioned among the Nityaklinnadēvatās of the *Lalitōpākhyāna*.

[2] Nirriti is the name by which this goddess of ill-luck, Alakshmī, the elder sister of Lakshmī, is mentioned in the *Padmōttarakhanda*. She is said to reside in the *pipal*-tree. Consequently also this tree is not to be touched except on Saturdays when, Lakshmī coming to see her sister, makes the tree auspicious.

[3] *South-Indian Inscriptions*, Vol. II, p. 60.

Fig. 135.—Jyēshṭhā ; Tiruvellavāyil.

for the goddess Durgā and one for Jyēshthā were caused to be made in that temple.[1] At Kukkanūr in the Nizam's Dominions, there is a celebrated Brahmanical temple dedicated to Jyēshthā. In Southern India her worship nowadays is much neglected, if not altogether avoided, she being supposed to be the goddess of misfortune and poverty.

X

In contrast to the ugly and fearsome goddesses mentioned above, there exist in the Hindu Pantheon other Saivite goddesses who are described as mild and extremely beautiful. Among these may be mentioned Bālā-Tripurasundarī of dazzling brilliance, "like a thousand suns bursting forth at the same time"; Saubhāgyabhuvanēsvarī, of red hue, a jewelled crown, a smiling face and heaving breasts, who holds a pot of gems in one hand and a red lotus in the other (fig. 136) and who places her right foot on a treasure of gems; Annapūrnā[2] of two or four arms who, in the former case, holds gracefully in one hand a jewelled vessel containing food and in the other a spoon to distribute the same (among her devotees), or in the latter, holds the noose and the hook in two hands and shows the protecting and the boon-giving postures in the others; the goddesses Gāyatrī,[3] Sāvitrī and

BĀLĀ-TRIPURASUNDARĪ. SAUBHĀGYABHUVANĒSVARĪ.

ANNAPŪRNĀ.

GĀYATRĪ, SĀVITRĪ and SARASVATĪ

[1] *Ind. Ant.*, Vol. XXII, p. 68. It may be noted that Mr. T. A. Gopinatha Rao in his *Elements of Hindu Iconography* (p. 391 f) considers the figures of Subrahmanya and his consorts worshipped in one of the chief rock-cut shrines of the temple to be Jyēshthā with her bull-faced son on one side and her fair daughter on the other. The figures are, indeed, much worn out and their features are indistinct; nor are the crow-banners characteristic of Jyēshthā, clearly visible. Two cocks, however, the banner of Subrahmanya, engraved on the rocky side walls of the same shrine and contemporaneous with the images, prove beyond doubt that the group is one of Subrahmanya and his two consorts and not of Jyēshthā. The shrine of the latter goddess, referred to in the inscription, is in a different compartment, in the lower storey of the same rock-cut temple. At Ānamalai, not far from Madura, is a similar rock-cut shrine of Subrahmanya but with only one goddess. The cock-banner of the god is, again, very clearly shown on the side walls, as in the Tirupparangunram shrine. People call it Sramanan-kōyil "the temple of Sramana (i.e., a Buddhist or a Jaina)" though the actual name must have been Saravanan-kōyil, "the temple of Saravanan" which latter name is connected with Saravanōdbhava, a synonym of Skanda-Subrahmanya.

[2] Literally, one who is full of food (to give to her devotees). This is the name of the famous goddess in Benares, who is also sometimes called Visālākshī, "the broad-eyed."

[3] Gāyatrī is of the nature of fire (or Brahmā), has four or ten arms and four faces and rides on a swan; Sāvitrī is of the substance of Rudra, has four arms, four faces, twelve eyes and the bull vehicle; Sarasvatī partakes of the nature of Vishnu, rides on Garuda, has four arms and one face and holds in her hands the Vaishnavite symbols, the discus, conch and the club as also the palm of protection.

FIG. 136.—Saubhāgyabhuvanēśvarī; Dhārāsuram.

Sarasvatī who preside over the morning, mid-day and evening prayers of the twice-born classes and represent the Vēdas, Rik, Yajus, and Sāman or the three sacred fires, *Gārhapatya*,

TULAJĀ-BHAVĀNĪ.

Dakshiṇāgni and the *Āhavanīya*, respectively; Tulajā-Bhavānī, who like Annapūrṇā holds in one hand a vessel of delicious food and in another a spoon for distributing the same;

RĀJA-MĀTANGĪ.

Rājamātangī who is absorbed in listening to the talk of a parrot and stands with one of her feet placed on a lotus, while her hands are fondly playing upon the *vīṇā*;

LAGHUSYĀ-MALĀ.

Laghusyāmalā, a damsel who has just attained her youth and who plays upon the *vīṇā*, with a vessel of wine near her and with eyes

VĀRUṆĪ.

betraying signs of intoxication; Vāruṇī, Sudhāmālinī or Amritēsvarī, "the goddess of boats," who is seated on a boat bedecked with gems and surrounded by an army of Saktis, bright as the growing sun, maddens the three worlds by her glance, decorates her tresses with the flowers of the *pārijāta*-tree and holds a vessel of wine, a lotus and a cooked piece

KURUKULLĀ.

of flesh in her hands; and Kurukullā,[1] also a goddess of boats, fully drunk with wine, riding on a boat of gems and

VINDHYAVĀ-SINĪ or MŪKĀMBIKĀ

holding in her hands a paddle of gems. Vindhyavāsinī,[2] classed as one of the Durgās, is called Mūkāmbikā in the *Silpasāra*. She is said to be seated on a golden lotus, to have four arms and to be dazzling as lightning. By her side stands the lion, her vehicle.

The most famous of these milder deities, however, are

LALITĀ, TRIPURA-SUNDARĪ and RĀJARĀJĒS-VARĪ.

Lalitā, Tripura-Sundarī and Rājarājēsvarī (fig. 137). All are highly beautiful and of dazzling brilliance. They have four hands each and hold the symbols: noose (or, fruit), goad (or, conch), sugarcane-bow (or, mirror) and five arrows (or, a lotus or a cup of collyrium). Their worship is directly connected with the mystic geometrical drawings known as *chakras* and *pīthas*. Images of these goddesses are not honoured so much as the *chakras* or *pīthas* over which they are supposed to preside. The worship offered consists in throwing over the *chakras* a profusion of red turmeric powder called *kuṅkumam*, which is generally worn on the forehead by all Hindu ladies whose husbands are alive. The throwing of *kuṅkumam* is accompanied by the repetition of long strings of the names of Lalitā consisting of synonyms—a thousand, three hundred, or one hundred and eight in number. Each name is prefaced with the sacred syllable *Ōm*. The goddesses

---

[1] This is a goddess common to both the Hindu and the Buddhist *Tantras*; *Mayūrabhañja*, p. lxxxix.

[2] In the Ankālamma temple at Kārempūdi (Guntūr district) is an inscription of A.D. 1164, which refers to that village goddess, as Vindhyavāsinī.

FIG. 137.—Rājarājēsvarī ; Rāmēsvaram.

are always presumed to be standing on a *chakra* imbedded in the earth and hence the worship is offered at the feet of the goddesses. In exceptional cases, however, as in the Kāmākshi-amman temple at Conjeeveram, the *chakra* is placed in front of the goddess. Bāla-Sakti, holding a book, rosary, goad and noose, is the presiding goddess of the six *chakras* as stated in the *Silpasāra*. The particular *yantra* sacred to her is known as *Bālā-yantra* which is described as a geometrical drawing having in its centre a dot (*bindu*) closed in by a triangle, a hexagon, a circle, a lotus of eight petals, a square and another square with openings at the cardinal points, consecutively. The *Sri-chakra* consisting of a larger number of intersecting triangles surrounded by circles and squares is another such mystic figure considered to be highly sacred to the goddess Lalitā. The latter is stated to have under her control innumerable fairy goddesses, some of whom are so delicate that they can enter, by the order of their mistress, into every atom of creation. Some with braided hair and beautiful *tilakas* of *kunkumam* on their foreheads are as sharp as fire and hold bows, arrows, swords and shields of flames. They are the personifications of almost every beneficent activity in the universe and are engaged in putting down the Evil Principle. Lalitā is said to have fought and killed, with the aid of these deities, several demons named Bhandāsura, Sumbha, Nisumbha, Chanda-Munda and Mahishāsura. All these, apparently, represent the powerfully persistent evil desires of men.

CHAPTER VI.

VILLAGE DEITIES.

I

Village deities and their relation to Tāntrik goddesses.

Most of the Saivite goddesses described above have been found to be of fearsome appearance, fond of flesh, blood and wine [1] and intimately connected with goblins, spirits, demons and diseases. One of them Tvaritā, it was seen, was the goddess of the Kirātas, and Vindhyavāsinī was evidently another living on the Vindhya Mountain. Āpyā (Durgā) is described in the *Harivamsa* as the goddess of the Sabaras, Pulindas, Barbaras and other wild tribes and as fond of wine and flesh. It will not now be difficult to trace a connexion between these and the village goddesses whose shrines are generally the haunts of malevolent demons and who are often appeased only by the slaughter of fowls, sheep, goats and buffaloes. Almost every village in South India, however insignificant it may be, has a shrine for one or more goddesses of this nature. Generally they are situated outside the village in groves of trees much dreaded by the people and are considered to be the *grāma-dēvatās,* the guardian deities of the village. Often there are no temples properly so called, and where there are structures, they are crude and simple enshrining within them rough unhewn stones representing the *amma* or "mother" sacred to that village. Sometimes there is only a spear or a trident fixed up straight in the ground in place of the goddess-stones. The goddesses bear different names. Some are called after the villages where their primary shrines exist, such as Kollāpuri-amma, Huskūr-amma, Pung-(i.e., Punganūr-)amma, Hosūr-amma, Uchchangi-amma, etc. Other popular names among village deities are the "Seven Kanniyamār," Bhadrakālī, Kāliyamma, Māriyamma, Mutyālamma, Ponnamma, Ellamma,[2] Ankālamma, Kolumamma,

---

[1] In the *Silpasāra*, where the Chaushashti-Yōginis are described, some are stated to feed on dead bodies, some to wander at nights like devils and some to be quarrelsome demons with ugly eyes and erect hair on head. Eighteen well-known shrines of these goddesses in India and Ceylon (Lankā) are enumerated.

[2] Nagendra Natha Vasu in his *Mayūrabhanja* speaks of a Greek goddess called Ellā and connects her with Ajaikapād, one of the forms of Rudra, already mentioned.

Selliyamma, Pattālamma, Vandi-Kāliyamma, Alagiyanāchchiyamma, Ulagāttāl, Pidāri, Pēchi, Kāttēri, Pōlēramma. Gangamma,[1] Chaudamma, Durgamma, Nūkalamma, Paidamma, Āsiramma, Pādālamma, Gontyālamma, Paradēsamma, Nēralamma, Mallamma, Peddintamma, Sōmalamma, Mātangirāla, Talupulamma, Sellāndiyamma, etc. Some of these names like Bhadrakālī, Kollāpuri-amma (Kollāpura-Mahālakshmī), Kāliyamma or Kālā-Pidāri (Kālī), Gangamma (Gangā), Chaudamma (Chandī ?), Durgamma (Durgā) and Mātangirāla (Mātangī, a recognized synonym of Pārvatī) are clearly mentioned in the *Tāntrik* works; and others can easily be traced to the same source. Māriyamma, for instance, under the name Mārikā occurs in the *Purānas* as the goddess presiding over small-pox and other infectious diseases. Kolumamma or Kulumāyamma, Selliyamma (Tsallamma of the Telugus) and Sellāndiyamma are evidently synonymous with Sītalā. Pōlēramma, the village goddess commonly worshipped in the Telugu country, is also supposed to correspond to Sītalā.[2] Peddintamma is perhaps Jyēshthā.

It is, however, difficult to explain similarly the origin of names like Ankālamma, Pattālamma, etc. Of these again, a few are of a flattering nature such as Mutyālamma, "the pearl-like mother" (fig. 138), Ponnamma or Bangāramma, "the golden mother," Alagiyanāchchiyamma, "the beautiful queen mother," etc. Ellamma probably means the goddess of boundaries (Telugu, *ella*).

Kālā-Pidāri and Durgā-Paramēsvarī of four arms are names of village goddesses which occur in early Chōla inscriptions. The shrines of these are generally termed *tirumurram.*[3] But sometimes, when they are structures, well endowed and

---

[1] In parts of the Guntūr district Gangamma is seen with the crocodile vehicle, e.g., at Pullagunta in the Palnad taluk. Evidently she represents the presiding deity of the river Ganges. In the epic poem *Rāmāyana*, where the heroine Sītā is made to worship the goddess Gangā (Ganges), she promises to offer, on her safe return from exile, fowls, buffaloes and wine to that goddess.

[2] Sītalā or Sītalādēvi is recognized as the goddess presiding over small-pox both in the Canarese and the Telugu districts.

[3] Rai Bahadur Venkayya describes Pidāri as a seated goddess with "fire issuing from her whole body to indicate her great wrath. On her head she wears a crown, various ornaments in her locks, on her forehead the mark of Siva, bulky jewels in the large holes of her ears and two flowers behind them. She has four hands holding in them, respectively, a kettle-drum with a snake, a trident, the skull of Brahmā and a goad. Her throne is an altar. Pidāri temples contain also an image of Vighnēsvara and the entrance is guarded by two horrible door-keepers called Mannadiyār. She has eighteen generals. Pidāri is said to be the chastizer of all evil spirits because those who hang or poison themselves, or die any violent death, are turned into malignant demons who would destroy the whole human race if not kept in check by Pidāri;" *S.I.I.*, Vol. II. Introduction, p. 41, note 1.

FIG. 138.—Mutyālamma; Āvani.

patronized like the other orthodox Hindu temples, they are called *srikōyil.* Four varieties of the goddess Pidāri are known from the records of Rājarāja I of the first quarter of the eleventh century A.D., viz., Punnaitturainangai, "the goddess (living on a river bank), in a grove of *punnai* trees," Poduvagai-ūr-udaiyāl, "the village deity common to all (classes)," Kuduraivattam-udaiyāl "the deity surrounded by (clay) horses," and Tiruvāl-udaiyāl, "the deity of the sacred banyan tree."

II

Worship of these deities.

The worship in the shrines of village goddesses is generally performed by non-Brahmans. In the Chingleput and North Arcot districts are a class of priests known as Ōchchans[1] who are exclusively devoted to service in Pidāri temples. They say that they are Brāhmanas of the Sākta creed and perform the worship according to the *Tāntrik* ritual. Sometimes, but very rarely, Brāhmanas also worship these fearful goddesses installed even within the sacred precincts of orthodox temples.[2] For example, Vattapirai-amman, "the mother who wears the circular crescent (on her head)" at Tiruvottiyūr near Madras, is a goddess of this kind to whom animal sacrifices are offered on fixed days in the year. On such occasions it is stated that the Sūdra priest takes the place of the usual Brāhmana and an entrance opening directly into the outer courtyard of the temple—kept closed on other days of the year—is now thrown open for the goddess to receive animal sacrifices and worship from her Sūdra or other devotees. After the annual festival is over, the goddess is purified. The buffalo sacrifices, which these village deities are generally fond of, indicate their connexion with Mahishāsuramardinī, the slayer of the buffalo-demon and with other similar *Tāntrik* goddesses mentioned above.

Peculiar ceremonies.

Some of the ceremonies peculiar to the temples of the village goddesses, besides animal sacrifices, are (1) fire-walking, (2) swinging on the *sidi* with a hook passed through the skin during what is otherwise known as the *chakra-pūjā*, (3) lashing oneself with a whip, (4) piercing a metallic wire right through the tongue or through the sides of the mouth, (5) slashing at the breast and forehead with swords until the blood

---

[1] Thurston's "Castes and Tribes," Vol. V, p. 419f.

[2] In many important Siva temples of the South, I have observed processional images of village goddesses kept in a separate room and worshipped. It is gathered from the priests of the temples that before commencing any important festivals in the Siva temple, these images are carried in procession and the village deities are first appeased, the expense being met from the Siva temple.

spurts out, (6) thrusting a spear through the abdomen[1] and (7) carrying on head the *karagam*, lamps of ghee, or earthen pots with blazing fire in them. Annual festivals called *jātras* are generally held in honour of the village deities. But when infectious diseases among men and cattle prevail, special worship is arranged for, to appease the deities by sacrificing animals, offering heaps of cooked rice mixed with blood, or by carrying the *karagam*. This last is celebrated by dressing the selected person who has taken a vow to perform the ceremony, in the yellow cloths of a woman, putting on him the ornaments of women and making him carry on his head a pot or pots profusely decorated with flowers and *margosa* leaves and supposed to contain in them the spirit of the particular goddess for whose propitiation the ceremony is gone through. A class of Tamil-speaking gardeners, called Tigalas in Mysore and allied to the Pallis or Vanniyans of other districts, are particularly devoted to the five Pāndavas of the *Mahābhārata* story, and to their common wife, Draupadī. The illustration from the courtyard of the Draupadī temple at Kumbakōnam (fig. 139) shows a group, in which the figure of Bhadrakālī with eight arms and a flaming crown, crushing the head of a giant under her left foot, is distinctly seen. The original goddess of the temple is, however, Draupadī whose metallic figure with that of Arjuna, one of her five husbands, is preserved in the central shrine. The two huge heads seen in the illustration, next to Bhadrakālī, are those of the hero, Aravan—said to be a son of Arjuna by a Nāga princess. He is believed to have been offered as a sacrifice on the great battle-field of Kurukshētra, especially with the object of securing success to the Pāndava brothers. Substantial big temples are built for Draupadī and the Pāndavas under the name Dharmarāja in the country round Kolar and Bangalore. The *karagam*-carrying ceremony is performed every year and attracts immense crowds of excited sightseers. The central figure of the ceremony is the priest who, as he madly trips along with the sacred weight over his head, like a high tiara decorated with flowers, is closely followed by a select number of men—the supposed attendant deities—with drawn swords in their hands. This scene very strongly reminds one of the goddess Sūlinī, who has been described above to be one of the *Tāntrik* goddesses,

DRAUPADĪ temples and *karagam*.

[1] Some of these inhuman practices seem to be but remnants of the older human sacrifices which were once quite a common feature of Sakti worship. Epigraphical evidence has been adduced to show that voluntary human sacrifices were offered even to the male deity Vīrabhadra (above, p. 161, footnote 2).

FIG. 139.—Group of images in the Draupadi-amman temple; Kumbakōnam.

followed by four unmarried girls with swords and shields in their hands or of a form of the goddess Durgā surrounded by maids with drawn swords. The Saptamātrikās of the *Tāntras* are also counted among village deities and are, perhaps, the same as "the Seven Kanniyamār (unmarried girls)" or the "Seven Sisters." They are frequently appeased by special worship when any unforeseen and sudden illness takes hold of a man. The local fortune-teller, often a woman of the *Korava* caste, being consulted, says that the patient is possessed by the "sisters" while walking alone in untimely hours of the day near tanks, gardens or groves. At once the goddesses are propitiated. A temporary shrine is constructed. Seven small stones are planted in a row, near a tank, almost touching the edge of the waters, and a small shed erected over them with leaves and flowers. Coconuts, plantains, fried rice and pulse are then offered to the stones and not unfrequently also a fowl. Even Brāhmanas worship the "Seven Sisters" in this way, but when a fowl is to be sacrificed they get a Sūdra to do it. The worship is enjoined to be performed in wet cloth after bathing.

Sati-worship and fire-walking ceremony.

The practice of honouring and even worshipping women who committed *sati* appears to have been very old in Southern India. Kannagi, the heroine of the Tamil poem *Silappadigāram*, died on hearing of the unjust death inflicted upon her husband by the Pāndya king of Madura. She was thenceforth worshipped in shrines built for her throughout Southern India and Ceylon. In the latter island she is known as Pattinī and is very popular. The mother of Rājarāja I is stated to have committed *sati* and in consequence of this act, evidently, an image of her was set up in the temple at Tanjore. Pērantālamma, a woman who committed *sati*, is equally reputed in the Telugu districts. Kanyakā-Paramēsvarī who is the tutelar deity of the Vaisya (Kōmati) caste is also connected with the story of a woman entering the sacred fire. The fire-walking ceremony peculiar to the temples of village goddesses may have some connexion with *sati*.

III

Aiyanār.

The village gods are not so many in number as the goddesses. Aiyanār, Hariharaputra or Mahā-Sāstā is supposed to be, as his name implies, a son of Siva and Vishnu.[1] When the celestial nectar was obtained by the *dēvas* and *asuras* after churning the ocean (see p. 139f, above) they quarrelled about

---

[1] For a fuller description of Aiyanār and his position among village deities, see *S.I.I.*, Vol. II, Introduction, p. 40, note.

the distribution of it. Vishnu assumed the form of a beautiful young woman, called Mōhinī, and by her attractions enticed the *asuras* and made them agree to depute her to distribute the precious liquid equally to all. She of course deceived them and gave the nectar to the gods alone. Siva saw Mōhinī at the time and was enamoured of her. He wedded her, and the result of their union was Hariharaputra. This deity is largely worshipped in Malabar and parts of Tinnevelly and Tanjore. In these districts he is not assigned the subordinate position of a village deity as in others. In the latter, however, he is one of the guardian deities of the village and, as such, is attended by *bhūtas* and *pisāchas*. He has long curly hair, a crown and ear-rings of gold-leaves. In his two arms he holds the bow and the arrow. He is dark of colour and is seated on a throne below a banyan tree. In the illustration given (fig. 140) the position of the hands of what is believed to be a figure of Aiyanār does not appear to suit the weapons, bow and arrow, which he is stated to hold.[1] In the figure from Valuvūr he is seen riding on an elephant in the very same posture, holding in his right hand what looks like a whip or an elephant goad (fig. 141). In front of his temple are placed figures of horses, elephants and other animals, made of wood or of painted brick and chunam, which are supposed to serve him as vehicles in his nightly perambulations. A third figure from Rāmēsvaram (fig. 142) represents him as riding on a horse. Pūranai and Pudgalai are stated to be his two wives, and Madurai-Vīran and Pāvādairāyan, his generals. Madurai-Vīran is a historical person whose adventures are noticed in the *South Arcot District Gazetteer*.[2] Kuttisāttan, Sāttan, Karuppan, Mundan and Gulikan are the names of some of the malignant demons that attend upon Aiyanār.

KARUPPANNASĀMI.

Karuppannasāmi is a similar god worshipped by the Kallars of Madura. Chains, clubs, spears and bill-hooks are his symbols; and these are presented by devotees at his shrines as votive offerings. They are generally found either hung on the trees or stuck into the ground. A similar god much dreaded by the people is Munīsvara whose name is quite popular. He is represented by a block of stone, a bush or sometimes a tree. Men and women called Muniyappa, Munisami, Muniyamma, etc., are so named because they were evidently born as the result of propitiating Munīsvara. It

---

[1] We have a similar figure of stone within the Natarāja temple at Chidambaram, which people call Ardhajāma-Alagar.

[2] Vol. I, p. 101.

FIG. 140.—Aiyanār (metal); Tiruppalātturai.

FIG. 141.—Aiyanār (metal) ; Valuvūr.

FIG. 142.--Aiyanār (metal); Rāmēsvaram.

might be noted that Buddha is called Muni in the lexicon *Amarakōsa* and that the forms of Siva known as Dakshināmūrti, Bhikshātana, Vīrabhadra, etc., are often those of wandering mendicants.

Deified heroes.

Heroes *(vīrulu)* who have given up their lives under romantic circumstances, in the cause of their native village or province, are also honoured as village deities and festivals are celebrated to propitiate them. Madurai-Vīran mentioned above was one of this kind. In the Palnād taluk of the Guntūr district, temples for heroes are quite a common feature.

Devil-dances.

Devil-dances in connexion with the annual festivals of village deities are common in Malabar and South Canara. The figures of the devils as represented by the Tuluva devil-dancers are described in detail with illustrative plates by Dr. Burnell in his article entitled "Devil Worship of the Tuluvas," in *Indian Antiquary*, Volumes XXIII and XXIV.

CHAPTER VII.

MISCELLANEOUS DEITIES.

I

Of the miscellaneous gods found in South-Indian temples, mention may be made of the Navagrahas or "the nine Planets" headed by the Sun. They are installed within the enclosed verandah round the central shrine of a temple with or without a special structure erected over them. The Sun stands in the centre and the others are fixed round him, each in a specified direction. The Planets are highly respected and scrupulously worshipped by the people, as they are believed to influence the destinies of human beings. NAVAGRAHAS.

II

The worship of the Sun in India has been as old as the Vēdas. Dr. Bhandarkar refers to a special class of sun-worshippers in the North called Magas whom he identifies with the Magi of ancient Persia.[1] In the South, there does not appear to be any such class exclusively devoted to the Sun. The worship is common to all. Āditya-grihas (Sun-shrines) are mentioned in inscriptions of the eighth and ninth centuries of the Christian era, in the northern districts of the Presidency; in later times temples of Traipurushadēva are found dedicated to Sun, Siva and Vishnu, with much prominence given to the first as indicated by the sculptures. Evidence of the building of separate Sun-temples in Southern India, earlier than the twelfth century A.D., has not yet been found. The only temple thus far known to be dedicated to the Sun and his attendant Planets exclusively, is the one at Sūriyanārkōyil in the Tanjore district.[2] SUN.

The image of the Sun-god, according to the *Āgamas*, is always to be placed in the centre of the Planets, looking eastward. Round, red, and decorated with red flowers, he must be clothed in garments of variegated colours with flags on his car. The car must have one wheel, drawn by seven

---

[1] *Vaishnavism*, *Saivism*, etc., pp. 151 to 155.

[2] Madras Epigraphical Report for 1908, Part II, paragraph 60.

horses and be driven by the charioteer Aruna who is represented without legs. The Sun is supposed to be a Kshatriya (sometimes, a Brāhmana) born of the sage Kasyapa. He is the lord of the Kalinga country,[1] wears a mail armour *(kavacha)* and robes in the northern fashion.[2] According to the Matsya-*Purāna*, he is represented seated (or standing) on a lotus seat, holding lotus flowers in his hands and is ever engaged in going round and round the mountain Mēru (fig. 143). His banner is the lion. This is the description of the Sun as the chief of Planets. But within the flaming Orb is recognized the god Nārāyana (Vishnu) whose body is golden, who assumes the forms of Brahmā in the morning, Mahēsvara (Siva)[3] in the midday and Vishnu in the evening. In this composite form he is seated on a lotus pedestal with crocodile ear-rings *(makara-kundala)* and a crown and exhibits in his hands the conch and discus and all the characteristic weapons of the Trimūrti. An illustration from Chidambaram (fig. 144) evidently represents Sūrya as composed of Brahmā, Mahēsvara and Vishnu, though the symbols held in the hands do not clearly indicate the same. On the pedestal are shown seven horses driven by Aruna, who, though believed to be without legs, is here represented with them.

Sūrya is also supposed to be the manifest form of the three Vēdas,[4] the sole supporter of universal space, resplendent in his car, surrounded by his consorts, Planets and the celestial damsels. Twelve different forms of the Sun (and sometimes thirty-two) are described, one having red light, another white light and so on. Hēmādri says that on the right and left sides of the Sun respectively, are represented the attendant gods Danda-Pingala and Ati-Pingala worshipping him, with pen and paper in their hands. His sons Rēvanta,[5] Yama and the two Manus and his four wives Rājnī, Svarnā, Chhāyā and Suvarchasā also stand on either side of him. It may be noted

---

[1] It may be noted that a famous temple of the Sun is at Konark in the Kalinga country.

[2] Varāhamihira's description of the images of the Sun is given by Dr. Bhandarkar on page 54 of his treatise on *Vaishnavism, Saivism*, etc. It is inferred from this that the dress worn by him must be non-Indian in its origin. The Avyanga which is also stated to encircle the Sun round his waist is identified with the Aivyaonghen of the Avesta language and is taken to signify the *kusti* worn by the Parsees of the present day.

[3] In the *Prayōgaratna* the Sun is invoked along with the gods Agni and Rudra. The former is described as the presiding deity of the Sun-god while the latter is the chief source of his energy.

[4] The seven horses of the Sun are accordingly interpreted to be the seven metres *(chhandas)* of the Vēdas.

[5] In inscriptions Rēvanta is quoted as the model of a superior horseman.

FIG. 143.—Sūrya ; Kumbakōnam.

FIG. 144.—Sūrya ; Chidambaram.

that a mystic diagram called the *Sūrya-yantra* is intimately connected with his worship as in the case of the Sakti goddesses. It is stated to be a circle bounded one after another, by a triangle, a circle, a square and two circles of eight and sixteen radii respectively.

III

Other Planets. The Moon is regarded as one of the Planets surrounding the Sun and going round and round the mountain Mēru. He is born of the Sea and of sage Atri and is supposed to be of the Vaisya caste. He is said to have only face and hands but no body. He turns towards the Sun, holds white lotuses in his two hands (or sometimes a club and the boon-conferring hand) and rides on a two-wheeled[1] chariot drawn by ten horses. Kuja (Mars) is a Kshatriya of Avantī, the son of the Earth and of sage Bharadvāja, wears red garments and a crown and has four arms in which are seen the weapons, club and *sakti* and the postures *varada* and *abhaya*. He faces the Sun and rides on a ram. Budha (Mercury), the son of the Moon, is a Vaisya of the Magadha country born in the lineage of Atri. He has four arms, a yellow body, and the lion vehicle. He shows in his hands the shield, club, *varada* and the sword and faces the Sun. Brihaspati (Jupiter) is a Brāhmana, born of Angiras. He comes from the Sindhu country and has either four or two arms, holding, in the latter case, the book and the rosary. He also faces the Sun. Sukra (Venus), likewise, is a Brāhmana born of Bhrigu and a native of Bhōjakata. According to Hēmādri he is seated in a golden chariot drawn by eight horses or in a silver chariot yoked to ten horses. He has two hands in one of which he holds a *nidhi* "treasure" and, in the other, a book. According to other authorities he has four arms in which are seen the staff, rosary, water-pot and the *varada*. Sani or Sanaischara (Saturn) is a Sūdra of the Saurāshtra country, and a descendant of Kasyapa, also facing the Sun. He is supposed to be born of the Sun, to have blue garments and to ride on a vulture or in an iron chariot drawn by eight horses. He is represented with two or four hands and stands on a lotus pedestal, but is more often found seated with four hands, his weapons being the arrow, trident and the bow. Rāhu and Kētu, the ascending and the descending nodes, are also represented as images (fig. 145). The former is described as a Sūdra of Paithan with a fearful face, black clothes and four arms, holding the sword, trident and the shield. He rides on a black lion and faces the Sun. Kētu is

[1] Some authorities say that the chariot is to be three-wheeled.

FIG. 145.—Rāhu and Kētu ; Chidambaram.

also a Sūdra, comes from Kusadvīpa and is born in the lineage of Jaimini. He has an ugly face, rides on a vulture and exhibits in his two arms the club and the *varada* posture.

IV

The next group of gods, frequently depicted though not as frequently worshipped as the Planets, are the Dikpālakas, "the eight lords of the quarters." These are mostly found represented on the central panel of the ceiling in the *Mahā-mandapa* of a temple. DIKPĀLAKAS.

Indra, the lord of the east, is the chief of them. He is a Vēdic god; the lord of all the minor gods. But he has long ago lost the high position assigned to him in Vēdic times. The story runs that he seduced Ahalyā,[1] the wife of sage Gautama, who cursed him for his lewdness to wear about his body marks of his lascivious conduct, but subsequently changed those marks into a thousand eyes dotted all over his body. Accordingly he is still known as "the thousand-eyed" *(Sahasr-āksha)*. Indra is represented with four arms riding on the celestial elephant Airāvata of four tusks (fig. 146). According to the *Silpasāra* the symbols which he presents are the bow, the protecting hand, the conch and the discus.[2] Hēmādri adds that his wife Sachī with two arms must be seated on his left thigh. In three of his hands he holds a lotus, goad and a thunderbolt, while the fourth passes round the back of Sachī. One of the arms of Sachī, likewise, is passed round the back of Indra, the other holding a bunch of flowers of the wish-giving tree *(kalpa-vriksha)*. INDRA.

Agni, the lord of the south-east quarter, is also one of the Vēdic gods and perhaps the most prominent of them. As the carrier of offerings to the various other gods in heaven, he plays an important part in the *Srauta* sacrifices and in the *Smārta* ceremonials, where fire oblations are essential. Every Brāhmana house-holder, strictly so called, is required to maintain the sacred fire in his house without quenching it and to offer oblations regularly three times a day, along with his usual prayers to Gāyatrī. Agni, as an image, is represented to be an old man; he is the oldest of the gods and a counterpart of the Sun on earth. He has a red body, two heads, six eyes, seven arms, seven tongues, four horns and three legs. AGNI.

---

[1] See also the *Journal of Indian Art and Industry*, No. 106, Plate 143, fig. 1020.

[2] The *Bhattabhāskarīya* mentions *abhaya*, *varada*, sword and the elephant goad.

FIG. 146.—Indra; Chidambaram.

He is surrounded by a circle of light, is seated on a lotus pedestal[1] and is supposed to reside in a quadrangle—evidently the quadrangular sacrificial fire-pit. In his seven arms he holds the vessels *prōkshanī* (sprinkler), *srik* (ladle), *sruva* (spoon), *pūrna-pātra* (vessel full of water), *tōmara* (pestle), fan and the ghee-pot, required in performing a sacrifice. He has braided hair, red garments and a big belly and wears the sacred thread *yajnōpavita*. His vehicle is the ram and his banner, the smoke issuing from the sacrificial fire-pit (fig. 146). He is attended on either side by his two wives Svāhā and Svadhā. Hēmādri describes him as having a single face, three eyes, moustaches and four arms. He rides in a chariot drawn by four parrots and driven by the god of winds, Vāyu. His wife Sāvitrī is seated on his left thigh, with a vessel of gems in her hand. In three of his arms Agni holds two flaming tridents and a rosary.

Yama, the lord of the south and the god of Death, has been already referred to in the description of the Siva image called Kālahā or Kālaharamūrti. He is dark of colour, exhibits the club, noose, *abhaya* and *varada* in his four arms and rides on a buffalo. The illustration from Chidambaram (fig. 148) shows only two hands in which are held the club and the noose. Hēmādri mentions as his symbols the staff, sword, a flaming trident and the rosary. His wife called Dhūmrōrnā is seated on his left thigh and holds a lime fruit in her left hand. To the right of Yama stand Chitragupta, Udīchya and others who keep a record of the actions of men. To his left stands the fierce Kāla with the death-noose in his hand. Two women called Dharmā "virtue" and Adharmā "vice" are seen on either side of Yama with *chauris* in their hands. YAMA.

Nairrita, the lord of the south-west region, is supposed to be the chief of the Rākshasas. He rides on a man, wields the mace and the javelin and has Kālikā for his wife. In the Kālikā-*Purāna* he is described as having two hands, holding a sword and shield and riding on an ass. He causes terror to demons, devils and spirits (fig. 149). NAIRRITA.

Varuna the regent of the west is also the lord of the ocean and of all aquatic animals. He has the crocodile vehicle and four arms. In the two upper hands he holds the serpent and the noose (fig. 150). According to Hēmādri he is seated in a chariot drawn by seven swans. In his four hands he holds the lotus, noose, conch and a vessel of gems and has VARUNA

[1] Or the half-moon seat *(ardhachandr-āsana)* according to the *Mayamata*.

FIG. 147.—Agni; Chidambaram.

FIG. 148.—Yama ; Chidambaram.

FIG. 149.—Nairrita Ahōbalam.

FIG. 150.—Varuna ; Lēpākshi.

an umbrella held over his head. The goddesses Gangā and Yamunā, holding *chauris* in their hands, stand on either side of him, the former riding on the crocodile and the latter on the tortoise.

VĀYU. Vāyu, the lord of the north-west, is blue in colour. In his hands are seen a fan, flag, *varada* and *abhaya*. He rides on a deer (fig. 151). An image of Vāyu at Chidambaram shows him only with two hands of which the right holds the flag and the left rests on the waist.

KUBĒRA. Kubēra, the lord of the north and the god of treasures, is a fat, ugly person as his name implies, but serene or self-satisfied and rides on a horse (fig. 152). Hēmādri describes him as riding on a man with his wife Riddhi[1] seated on his left thigh. He is the chief of the demi-gods called Yakshas and Kinnaras. Two treasures personified, viz., Sankhanidhi and Padmanidhi, are supposed to attend upon him on either side. He is the friend of Siva the lord of the adjoining north-east quarter.

V

Nāgas. The worship of the "serpents" (Nāgas)[2] is prevalent all over India and particularly so in the west coast of the Madras Presidency, where a corner of a house or of a field is exclusively dedicated to the living cobra so that it may dwell there with its family group. In other parts of the Presidency on a particular day of the year sacred to the Nāgas, milk, fruit and coconut are placed near a snake-hole with the object of feeding the cobra. Nāga-images cut on stones as plain serpents with one, three, five, seven or nine hoods, are also worshipped. Sometimes these have a human body above the navel and a serpent's coils below. Female snakes are said to have one hood only.

Snake-stones are installed in temples and other places, on specially prepared platforms under the shade of the *pipal* and the margosa trees. A ceremony called "the marriage of the *pipal*-tree" is performed both by Brahmans and non-Brahmans, when Nāga stones are also fixed under these trees amidst great rejoicing. The connexion of the Nāgas with the *pipal* and the margosa trees is evidently a relic of the ancient tree and serpent worship. Serpents have been worshipped in India from very early times, earlier even, perhaps, than the

[1] The *Bhattabhāskariya* calls her Chitrinī.

[2] It is mentioned in the Buddhist *Niddesa* among the various systems of belief and superstition that prevailed in the fourth century B.C. (Dr. R. G. Bhandarkar's *Vaishnavism, Saivism*, etc., p. 3).

FIG. 151.—Vāyu ; Lēpākshi.

FIG. 152.—Kubêra; Lêpâkshi.

Vēdic Sun, Moon and Brahmā. It is believed that a propitiation of the Nāgas conduces towards the production of children. This belief may be traced in other countries also, where there are signs of the once widely prevalent serpent worship. Eight lords of Nāgas are mentioned in the *Āgamas*. The chief of these is Ananta, Sēsha or Ādisēsha, on whose folds Vishnu is supposed to sleep. Fig. 153 represents him in a semi-human form. In an inscription of the twelfth century A.D. the eight Nāgas, Sēsha, Vāsuki, Takshaka, Karkōtaka, Abja (Padma), Mahāmbuja (Mahā-Padma), Sankhadhara and Kulika are invoked to decide about the auspicious or inauspicious nature of the grant.[1]

Besides the Nāgas mentioned in the previous paragraph, there are other groups of demi-gods and demons largely depicted in Hindu temples, such as the Yakshas, Vidyādharas, Gandharvas, Apsarasas, Kinnaras and Rākshasas.[2] These are made to serve, generally, as *chauri*-bearers to the gods and are represented with a light body flying in the air. They have generally two hands, two eyes and the *karandamakuta* crown. The *Mānasāra* describes the Kinnaras as having the legs of a cock the middle part of their body being human and the face beaked like Garuda with spreading wings. They wear a crown on their heads and hold a *vīnā* in their arms. A sketch from Rāmēsvaram illustrates a female Kinnarī (fig. 154). The origin and description of these groups of demi-gods are given by W. J. Wilkins in Chapter XI of his *Hindu Mythology*. Also, the figures of these in their various postures are beautifully illustrated in the rock sculptures known as "Arjuna's Penance" at Mahābalipuram.

Yakshas, Vidyādharas Gandharvas, etc.

The Dvārapālas seen at the entrance into almost every Hindu shrine are also demi-gods and bear different names being sometimes called Chanda and Prachanda, sometimes Jaya and Vijaya, or Harabhadra and Subhadra according as they occupy the second, third or fifth door-way opening into the shrine. In the standing figures of Dvārapālas the right leg is placed straight on the pedestal *(svastika)* and the left is slightly bent *(kunchita)*. The posture of their body may be: (1) with legs and back partly turned to front; (2) hands resting on the thigh which then is bent in the shape of a plough; or (3) with both hands supporting the *gōpura*. The *Silpasangraha* states that in form the Dvārapālas are like *bhūtas* with two big hands in one of which they hold a club. They

Dvārapālas.

---

[1] Madras Epigraphical Report for 1910, p. 117, para. 60.

[2] See *Visvakarma*, Part V, plate 66.

FIG. 153.—Ādisēsha ; Chidambaram.

FIG. 154.—Kinnarī ; Rāmēsvaram.

have protruding canine teeth, when Saiva, and narrow waists; are beautiful in form, but disfigured in the face (fig. 155).[1] Figures of Dvārapālas are sometimes also found to have four arms and to hold the Saiva or the Vaishnava symbols according as they are placed in Siva or Vishnu temples. The fine image (fig. 156) of a Dvārapāla from Dhārāsuram, Tanjore district, which has four arms and is probably Saiva, is stated to have been brought as a trophy from Kalyānapura (i.e., Kalyāna in the Nizam's Dominions), by the Chōla king Rājādhirāja I, in the middle of the eleventh century A.D. Entrances into the shrines of goddesses are attended by Dvārapālikās just as those of the gods are guarded by Dvārapālas.

VI

Saints and Sages.

Saints and Sages are also not infrequently figured in temples. The latter include the Vēdic *rishis* and the authors of the early sacred literature of the Hindus, represented as old men, serene and unmindful of mundane affairs. The sacred thread, braided hair, flowing beards and moustaches form the special features of *rishi* images. They are seated in a meditative posture with the rosary or book and the water-pot or staff in their hands. The seven famous sages Gautama, Bharadvāja, Visvāmitra, Kasyapa, Jamadagni, Vasishtha and Atri are occasionally also represented with their wives, while

NĀRADA. AGASTYA.

Nārada, Agastya, Bhrigu, Angiras, etc., are surrounded by their disciples. Nārada (fig. 157) is distinguished from other sages by the *vīnā* which he holds in his hands, being always engaged in singing the praises of Vishnu. In *Purānas* he is described as fond of setting up one against the other and creating quarrels. Hence in common parlance Nārada represents a tale-bearer. Agastya (fig. 158) is dwarfish in stature and pot-bellied.[2] He is supposed to have migrated from north to south and to have dwelt there permanently and developed the Tamil language of which he is said to be the

KAPILA.

first grammarian. Kapila, the founder of the Sānkhya system of Hindu philosophy, holds a water-pot on his lap and has

DHANVANTARI.

in his two hands the conch and the discus.[3] Dhanvantari,

[1] In the *Silpasāra* the Dvārapālas of Siva temples are stated to be Nandi and Mahākāla at the eastern entrance; Bhringi and Vināyaka at the southern entrance; the sacred Bull and Skanda at the western entrance and Chandi at the northern.

[2] A bronze illustration from Nallūr is given in the Madras Archæological Survey Report for 1911-12, Plate A, fig. 2.

[3] In *Visvakarma*, Part I, Plate 52, a totally different form of Kapila, from Ceylon, is given. Perhaps he is not identical with the sage described here.

FIG. 155.—Dvârapâla ; Tiruvottiyûr.

FIG. 156.—Dvārapāla ; Dhārāsuram.

FIG. 157.—Nárada; Chidambaram.

FIG. 158.—Agastya; Chidambaram.

the presiding sage of the Indian Medical Science, is supposed to be a form of Vishnu and is found generally figured in company of the Asvins,[1] who are the physicians of the gods. He holds a pot of nectar in his hands.

Among the human beings who have attained sainthood may be included the great religious reformers such as Sankarāchārya, Rāmānujāchārya, Madhvāchārya and others. The first is represented as a *sannyāsin* (mendicant) with a bald head and a body besmeared with ashes. He holds a book in his left hand and shows the *chinmudrā*, the teaching pose of fingers, in the other. The staff and the water-pot *(kundikā)* which are the symbols of the *sannyāsins*, are found placed by his side. Seated on the tiger's skin in the *padmāsana* posture he is surrounded by attendant pupils. Sankarāchārya may also be found decorated with a necklace of *rudrāksha*-beads which are sacred to Siva. The illustration from Tiruvottiyūr (fig. 159) shows Gaulīsvara (Gaudapāda ?), the teacher's teacher of Sankarāchārya, with four arms, occupying the highest seat. Below him to the right is Sankarāchārya and below him on the pedestal are depicted the latter's four pupils. Rāmānujāchārya has the *sānjali-mudrā*, i.e., hands folded together over the breast in a worshipping posture, the triple staff *(tridanda)* and a head-dress. He wears the Vaishnava caste marks *ūrdhvapundra* (or *nāmam*) made of white clay and red pigment (fig. 160 *(d)*). Vēdānta-Dēsika (fig. 160 *(b)*) is also a Srī-Vaishnava teacher of great fame. Madhvāchārya, like Sankara, is a bald-headed *sannyāsin* with the *chinmudrā*, the book, the staff and the *kundikā*. He wears the caste mark *ūrdhvapundra* and the Vaishnava symbols of conch, discus, etc., made on his body either of sandal-paste or of the yellow clay called *gōpichandana*.

SANKARA-CHĀRYA.

RĀMĀNUJĀ-CHĀRYA and VĒDĀNTA-DĒSIKA.

MADHVĀ-CHĀRYA.

Saiva and Vaishnava saints (called *Nāyanārs* and *Ālvārs*), the former of whom are sixty-three in number and the latter twelve are also occasionally installed in temples, their images being made either of metal or of stone. The most famous of the former are Appar, Sundarar and Tirujnānasambandar,[2]

Saiva and Vaishnava Saints.

[1] These are the two gods Nāsatya and Dasra mentioned in the Vēdas. They are of the form of a horse except in their faces and are found together, seated on the same lion-pedestal. In two of their arms they exhibit the *abhaya* and the book. On their right are represented the medical herbs *Mritasamjīvani* and *Visalyakarani* and on their left, the sages Dhanvantari and Ātrēya (?).

[2] In the Madras Archæological Survey Report for 1911–12, Plate 11, figs. 1–4, are given illustrations of four bronze images which represent Appar, Mānikkavāsagar, Jnānasambandar and Sundarar (?). *Visvakarma*, Part IV, Plates 62 and 63, illustrate figures of Mānikkavāsagar and Sundaramūrti (Sundarar) from Ceylon. Havell gives a picture of Appar (*Ideals of Indian Art*, Plate XIV). In the

FIG. 159.—Gaulisvara (Gaudapâda ?) and Sankarâchârya ; Tiruvottiyûr.

FIG. 160 (metal).—(*a*) Garuda; (*b*) Vēdanta-Dēsika; (*c*) Vishvaksēna; (*d*) Rāmānujāchārya; (*e*) Tirumangai-Ālvār; Nāmakkal.

whose devotional hymns in praise of the many Saiva shrines of the South are collected together under the name *Dēvāram* and are regarded as scriptures by the devout section of the Saivas. Stories relating to the pious lives of the sixty-three Saiva devotees are recorded in the book called *Periyapurāṇam*, which was written about the end of the thirteenth century of the Christian era. Māṇikkavāsagar, the author of the *Tiruvāsagam*, is also a saint of great reputation. A beautiful image of his (fig. 161) comes from Tiruvarangulam in the Pudukkōttai State. An illustration from Madura (fig. 162) of Kāraikkāl-Ammai, one of the female Saiva saints counted among the sixty-three, gives a true picture of how devotion and severe penance are expected to reduce the physical body to a skeleton. Like the Saiva scriptures, the hymns of the Vaishnava saints (*Ālvārs*) (see Tirumangai-Ālvār, fig. 160 (*e*) above), are also collected under the name *Nālāyiraprabandham* and form the accredited scriptures of the Tengalai section of Srī-Vaishnavas. The lives of the *Ālvārs* are given in the book entitled *Guruparamparāprabhāva*.

Numerous other images are mentioned in the *Āgamas*, *Purāṇas* and similar other works. These are rarely, if at all, depicted in temples. The nine Prajāpatis, the eight Vasus, the seven (or sometimes forty-nine) Maruts, the ten Visvēdēvas, the fourteen Manus, the nine Chiranjīvins, are all personified and described with their weapons and vehicles. Even the sixty-four sciences, the sixty years of the cycle, the months, fortnights, days, constellations, signs of the zodiac, seasons, solstices, oceans, quarters, mountains, rivers, etc., are similarly personified and described. It is not necessary to consider them in any detail.

VII

The Digambara Jaina images.

A brief description may now be given of the Digambara Jaina images, of which we have a good number in the districts of Chingleput, South Arcot, South Canara and other parts of the Madras Presidency. It is not possible to enter here into a detailed enquiry of Jaina ritual, symbolism, idology, etc. We

---

Tanjore temple built by Rājarāja I at the beginning of the eleventh century A.D., were installed images of Nambi-Ārūranār (i.e., Sundaramūrti), Tirujnānasambandar, Nangai-Paravaiyār (wife of Sundaramūrti), Tirunāvukkaraiyar, Periya-Perumāl and his queen Lōkamahādēviyār, Meypporul-Nāyanār and Siruttonda-Nāyanār. The set of images illustrating the story of the last-mentioned, included Kshētrapāla, Bhairava, Siruttonda-Nambi, Tiruvenkāttu-Nangai (his wife) and Sīrāladēvar (his son); see *S.I.I.*, Vol. II, Introduction, p. 39 f. In the temple at Dhārāsuram near Kumbakōnam are pictured scenes from the lives of most of these sixty-three Saiva devotees with labels cut on their pedestals. These belong to the thirteenth century A.D.

FIG. 161.—Mânikkavâsagar (metal); Tiruvarangulam.

FIG. 162.—Kāraikkāl-Ammai ; Madura.

may simply note what the Hindu *Silpa-Sāstras* say about them. The general description of Jaina images, as supplied by these works, is that they must have long arms so as to reach the knees, the mark of *Srivatsa* on the breast (which was found to be peculiar to Vishnu), a calm countenance, broad forehead, head covered with starry rings of hair, hanging earlobes, high nose, delicate limbs and a naked body which looks young and beautiful. Figures of Arhantadēva (i.e., a Jaina Saint) may be made movable or immovable, standing or seated. The material used must be the white, red, yellow, or black stone, crystal or metal. Whether standing or seated the images must have a straight back and in the latter case, the *padmāsana* or the *siddhāsana* posture with the hands crossed over the lap palm in palm, the right being below and the left above. The pedestal of Jaina Saints is always a *simhāsana*, "lion-seat," surmounted by a "crocodile-aureola" *(makara-tōrana)* fixed at the back of the image. Over the aureola are depicted the *kalpa*-tree, the Indras and Dēvas, the demi-gods of Jaina mythology. Sometimes there may also be sages (like Nārada) attending upon the Jina and Yakshas, Yakshis, Vidyādharas, Chakravartins, Nāgēndras and Dikpālakas holding *chauris*, on either side of him. Images used by the Jainas in daily worship at home or in Mathas include the *Panchaparamēshthins* who wear neither clothes nor jewels. At the entrance into the shrines of Jina are placed the gate-keepers Chanda and Mahā-Chanda, as in Hindu temples. Jainas are divided into two main divisions, the Svētāmbaras and the Digambaras. The former are not found in the south while the latter have their important seats at Sravana-Belgola in the Mysore State, Mūdbidri, Kārkal and Yēnūr in South Canara, Tirumalai near Pōlūr in North Arcot, Sittāmūr in South Arcot and various other places. A descriptive account of the images of Digambara Jainas with illustrative plates has been given by Dr. Burgess in his article entitled "Digambara Jaina Iconography" in *Indian Antiquary*, Vol. XXXII, pp. 45 ff. It shows that the gods and goddesses of the Jainas are as numerous and as richly conceived as those of the Hindu Pantheon, and have their prescribed weapons, jewellery, vehicles and symbols.

VIII

In concluding this small treatise on South Indian gods and goddesses, it will not be out of place to dwell briefly upon the pedestals, postures, symbols, weapons and jewellery of images, although most of these have been noticed where they occur incidentally, in the above pages.

Pedestals. The *Mayamata*, speaking of pedestals in general, says that they are triangular, half-moon-shaped, square or circular (?).[1] Nine pedestals *(pithas)* are mentioned by name, viz., *bhadrapitha*, *vajrapitha*, *padmapitha*, *māhāmbuja* (the big lotus), *srikara*, *pithapadma*, *mahāvajra*, *saumyaka*, and *srikāmya*. Of these, the first and the third are pictured on the accompanying Plate I, as Nos. 13 and 12. No. 16 on the same Plate, perhaps, represents *mahāmbuja*.

Postures. The postures, symbols and weapons of images differ according as the image is conceived to be either in a fighting attitude or as bestowing bliss and knowledge on its worshippers. Sometimes, even though the weapons of war are exhibited in the hands of an image, it may yet be considered peaceful if it only shows the positions of the hands known as *abhaya* and *varada*. The posture, *sukhāsana*, in a seated image (Plate I, No. 14) and the posture *samapādasthānaka* in a standing image (Plate II, No. 4) are generally adopted in conferring bliss, just as the position of the hands *abhaya* (Plate IV, No. 7) and *varada* (Plate III, No. 23) indicate the same. The *ālidha*[2] (Plate II, Nos. 5 and 6) and the *utkatika*[3] postures (Plate I, No. 15) denote respectively the heroic attitude in actual fighting and the angry mood that immediately follows it. The *padmāsana* (Plate I, No. 16) and the *yōgāsana* (Plate II, No. 1) postures show either the meditative or the teaching attitude. The position of the legs (Plate II, Nos. 2 and 3) adopted in the case of the standing images of Gōpāla and Natarāja show not only a graceful and artistic attitude but, evidently, also indicate the ecstasy of joy. It may be noted that in all figures of gods and goddesses standing in any position, the ideal beauty is recognized to consist in the three *bhangas* (bends) which according to the *Silpasangraha* are *ābhanga* (slight bend), *samabhanga* (medium bend) and *atibhanga* (great bend). Each of these three bends may be found separately or together in one and the same image.[4]

---

[1] According to the *Prayōgaratna* the nine Planets are to be seated on circular, quadrilateral, triangular, arrow-shaped, rectangular, pentagonal, bow-shaped, winnow-shaped and flag-shaped pedestals.

[2] The *ālidha* posture is assumed generally in drawing the bow and discharging the arrow.

[3] There is reason to suppose that the posture known as *virāsana* wherein one leg has to be placed on the other so as to rest on that thigh, is sometimes substituted for *utkatika*. Perhaps they are synonymous.

[4] See *South Indian Bronzes* by O. C. Gangoly, p. 401f. The *Silpasangraha* describing a particular form of Kāma states that it consists of three *bhangas* or bends, the face slightly leaning to the right, the middle of the body to the left and the portion below the waist, again, to the right.

The symbols of the gods and goddesses apart from the weapons which they wield, such as the goad (Plate IV, No. 8), noose (No. 9), disc (Nos. 10 and 10*a*), shield (No. 12), sword (No. 13), pestle (No. 14), axe (No. 15), trident (Nos. 16 and 16*a*), thunderbolt (Nos. 20 and 20*a*), club (Plate III, No. 1), *sakti* or *vēl* (No. 2), *tanka* (No. 3), arrow (No. 4), bow (No. 5), fire (No. 6) and *khatvānga* (No. 11), are very few. Goddesses, perhaps as a sign of beauty, hold in their hands a lotus-bud (Plate IV, No. 18 and Plate I, No. 3), a mirror (Plate III, No. 8) or a parrot perching on the back of the palm (Plate IV, No. 19). The rosary (Plate IV, Nos. 1 and 2), the water-pot (Nos. 3 and 4), the book (No. 5), the position of the fingers known as *chinmudrā* (Plate III, No. 16) and *jnānamudrā* (No. 14) denote meditation, purity and knowledge. The conch of Vishnu (Plate IV, No. 11 and Plate I, No. 4*a*), the kettle-drum *dhakkā* of Siva (Plate III, No. 12 and Plate IV, No. 24) and the bell in the hands of some gods and goddesses (Plate III, No. 7) may be taken as equipments for fight, though not as actual weapons, offensive or defensive. The deer held by Siva as a trophy on the occasion when he destroyed the sacrifice of his father-in-law Daksha (Plate IV, No. 17), the serpent (Plate I, No. 46) and the *kapāla* (Plate III, No. 21 and Plate IV, No. 23*a*) may be considered only as symbols specially distinguishing him from the other gods. The same has to be said of the *kukkuta* "cock" (Plate III, No. 3*a*) of Skanda, of the broken tusk[1] (Plate IV, No. 21) of Vināyaka and of the flag (No. 22) of Vāyu, "the god of winds."

Symbols and weapons.

Some of the purely artistic positions of the hand are: the *simhakarna* (Plate I, No. 1), the *kataka* (Plate IV, No. 4*a*), the *katiga* "hand resting on the waist" (Plate IV, No. 6), the position in which the hand hangs down freely "like the tail of a cow" (Plate I, No. 2), the placing of the *kūrpara* by Siva on the head of the bull (Plate III, No. 9), the *gajahasta* of Natarāja (No. 19) and the position in which Siva as Bhikshātana touches the mouth of the antelope (Plate III, No. 17).[2] Some other significant positions of the hand are those known as *sūchi* "the pointing finger" (Plate III, No. 13 and Plate IV, No. 23), *tarjani* "the threatening finger" (Plate III, Nos. 18 and 26) and the *vismaya* "wonder" (Plate III, Nos. 15 and 22 and Plate I, No. 4). The three latter are generally found in the figures of Siva and of guardian deities.

Positions of the hand.

[1] For the story of the broken tusk with which Vināyaka (Ganapati) is stated to have written the *Mahābhārata*, see above, p. 176.

[2] This last position is called *simhakarna*. In images of Tripurāntakamūrti, the arrow is held by one of the right hands which is, again, stated to be in the *simhakarna* pose.

Jewellery, crowns, etc.

The jewellery of images corresponds in most cases to the jewels of the present day worn by men as well as by women. Most of these have been mentioned in the above pages in the general descriptions of gods and goddesses. It has only to be noted that a very large number of them, such as necklaces, breast-plates, girdles, armlets, bracelets, wristlets, anklets, arm-rings, finger-rings, and toe-rings, made of gold and set with various gems,[1] are mentioned in the Tanjore inscriptions as having been presented to the images in the Brihadīsvara temple, by the great Chōla king Rājarāja I, in the first quarter of the eleventh century A.D. The different fashions of making up the hair seem to have also occupied the attention of Indian artists. The *jatās* (matted hair) of Siva, arranged generally in the form known as *jatāmakuta* (Plate I, No. 8), show other varieties such as *jatāmandala* (Plate II, No. 6), *jatābhāra* (No. 9) and *jatābandha* (No. 7). The terrible form of Siva, known as Pāsupatamūrti, has the *jatāmakuta* with flames of fire surrounding it (Plate I, No. 11). Natarāja's *jatās*, whether flying in the air or tied up in a knot have a bunch of peacock's feathers decorating them (Plate I, No. 5). Vishnu has generally a *kirītamakuta*, i.e., a crown (Plate I, No. 7). The goddesses either wear the crown called *karandamakuta* (Plate II, No. 8)[2] or have their hair parted in the middle like the Indian women of to-day. In figures of Jyēshthā, is seen a peculiar fashion of dressing the hair known as *vāsikābandha* (Plate I, No. 10). Other peculiar head-dresses, whose names are not known, also occur occasionally (see, e.g., Plate I, No. 9).

---

[1] See above p. 8, fig. 4. One of the peculiar jewels worn by images of Siva such as Natarāja, Dakshināmūrti, Bhikshātana, Kankāla, etc., is the *bhringipāda* (Plate II, Nos. 3 and 4). It may be noted that the priestly class among Lingāyatas, called Jangams, wear such a jewel when they go out for receiving doles.

[2] When represented independently and in a fighting or otherwise terrible attitude, they may wear the *jatāmakuta* like male deities.

Gandabherunda.

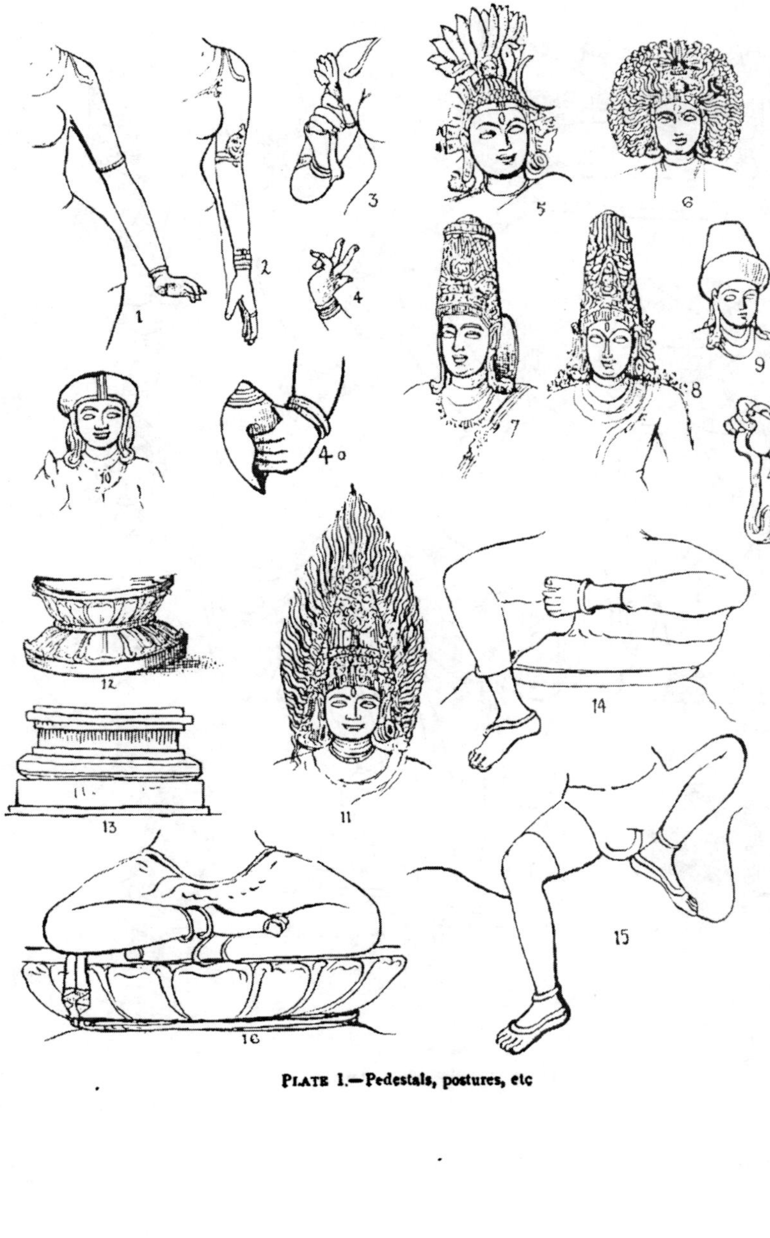

PLATE I.—Pedestals, postures, etc

PLATE II.—Pédestals, postures, etc.

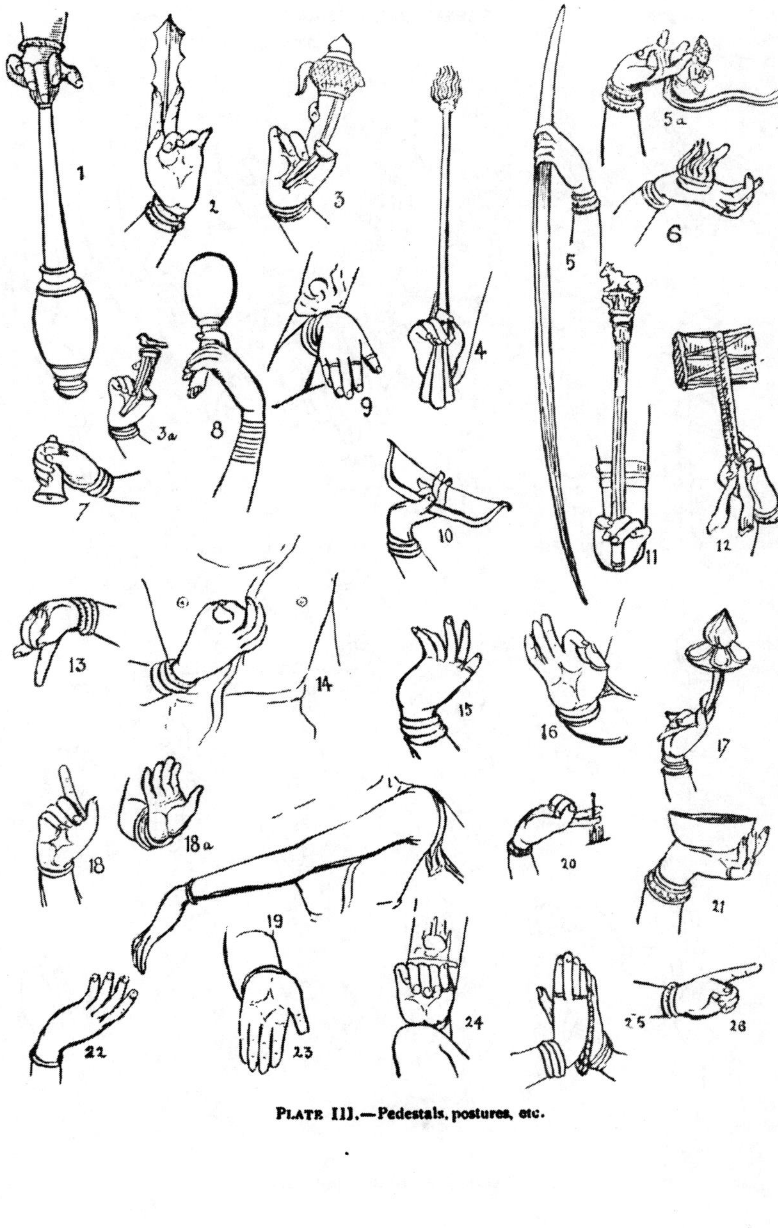

PLATE III.—Pedestals, postures, etc.

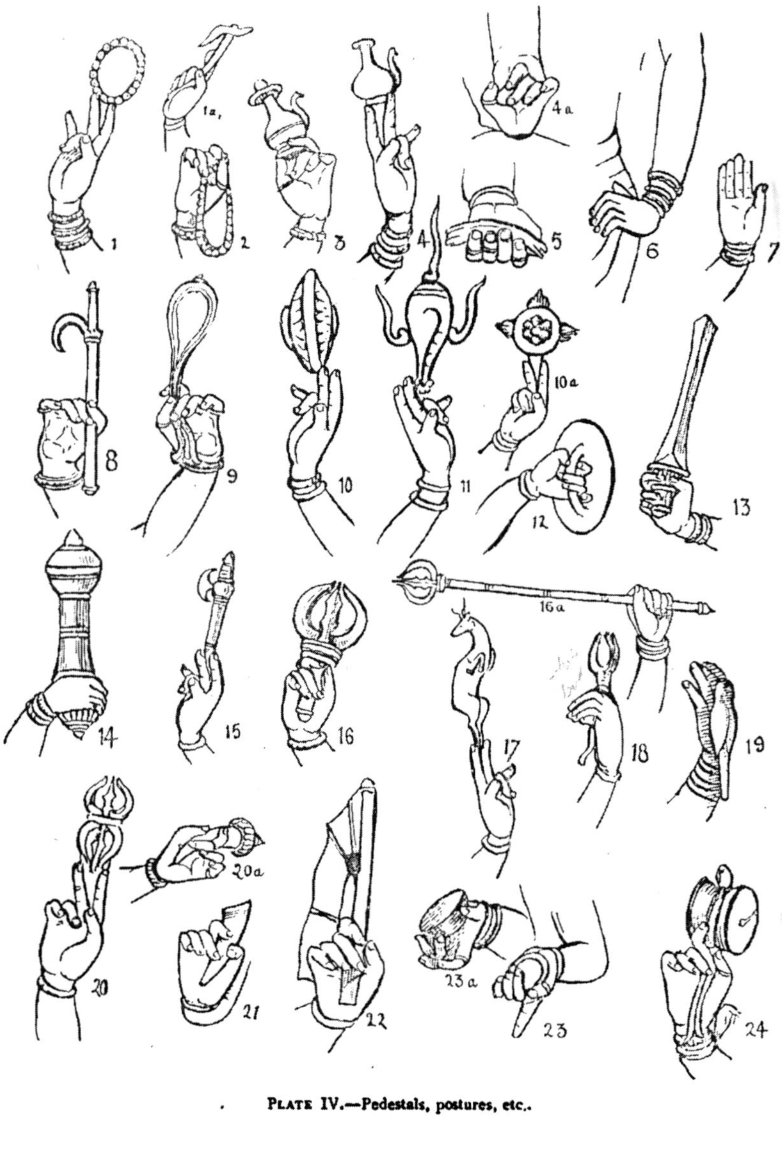

PLATE IV.—Pedestals, postures, etc.

INDEX.

[*Note:* Figures after articles refer to pages; the following abbreviations are used:— *n.* = footnote; *s.a.* = same as; *do.* = ditto; *q.v. (quod vide)* = which see.]

A

C

D

E

F

G

U

V

W

Y